high fiber
cooking for health

high fiber
cooking for health

over 50 delicious recipes for healthy
eating that are high in dietary fiber

anne sheasby

southwater

This edition is published by Southwater

Southwater is an imprint of Anness Publishing Ltd
Hermes House, 88–89 Blackfriars Road, London SE1 8HA
tel. 020 7401 2077; fax 020 7633 9499
www.southwaterbooks.com; info@anness.com

UK agent: The Manning Partnership Ltd, 6 The Old Dairy, Melcombe Road, Bath BA2 3LR;
tel. 01225 478444; fax 01225 478440; sales@manning-partnership.co.uk

UK distributor: Grantham Book Services Ltd, Isaac Newton Way,
Alma Park Industrial Estate, Grantham, Lincs NG31 9SD;
tel. 01476 541080; fax 01476 541061; orders@gbs.tbs-ltd.co.uk

North American agent/distributor: National Book Network, 4501 Forbes Boulevard,
Suite 200, Lanham, MD 20706;
tel. 301 459 3366; fax 301 429 5746; www.nbnbooks.com

Australian agent/distributor: Pan Macmillan Australia, Level 18, St Martin's Tower,
31 Market St, Sydney, NSW 2000;
tel. 1300 135 113; fax 1300 135 103; customer.service@macmillan.com.au

New Zealand agent/distributor: David Bateman Ltd, 30 Tarndale Grove, Off Bush Road, Albany, Auckland;
tel. (09) 415 7664; fax (09) 415 8892

A CIP catalogue record for this book is available from the British Library.

Publisher: Joanna Lorenz
Project Editor: Zoe Antoniou
Designer: Ian Sandom
Photographer: David Jordan
Additional Photographers: Janine Hosegood (pp8, 10, 12 left) and Patrick McLeavey (pp12 right, 13)
Illustrator: Madeleine David
Stylist: Judy Williams

Previously published as Healthy Eating Library *The High Fiber Cookbook*

1 3 5 7 9 10 8 6 4 2

NOTES

Bracketed terms are intended for American readers.

For all recipes, quantities are given in both metric and imperial measures and,
where appropriate, measures are also given in standard cups and spoons.
Follow one set, but not a mixture, because they are not interchangeable.

Standard spoon and cup measures are level.
1 tsp = 5ml, 1 tbsp = 15ml, 1 cup = 250ml/8fl oz

Australian standard tablespoons are 20ml.
Australian readers should use 3 tsp in place of 1 tbsp
for measuring small quantities of gelatine, flour, salt, etc.

Medium (US large) eggs are used unless otherwise stated.

CONTENTS

INTRODUCTION

The importance of fibre in a healthy, balanced diet should not be underestimated. Once labelled "roughage" and thought of simply as a bulking agent, dietary fibre is increasingly seen as essential in preventing or at least alleviating a wide range of digestive disorders and is believed to be implicated in lowering cholesterol levels and helping to prevent coronary heart disease.

Western man has gone soft – in dietary terms – swapping a diet that was traditionally high in fibre for one which relies heavily on processed low-fibre foods. It has been estimated that many of us consume no more than 11g of fibre a day, whereas the recommended daily intake is between 12 and 18g.

This book looks at all the advantages of increasing the amount of dietary fibre we consume, and suggests a few simple changes which can be introduced over time to make a healthy, well-balanced diet even better. It includes a selection of tempting recipes, chosen first for flavour, second for fibre-content and always for all-round appeal to every member of the family.

THE IMPORTANCE OF FIBRE

Changing to a diet that is higher in dietary fibre is not difficult, but it should be done gradually. Sudden and significant changes to your normal eating patterns may actually upset the digestive system.

Dietary fibre – or non-starch polysaccharides (NSP), as it is more accurately described – is divided into two main types: soluble fibre and insoluble fibre. As the name suggests, soluble fibre dissolves in water to form a soft, gooey liquid or gel that can be fermented by the bacteria in the gut and absorbed by the body. Soluble fibre is found in oatmeal, pulses such as lentils, fruits such as oranges and bananas and some vegetables, especially sweetcorn and green, leafy vegetables.

Insoluble fibre cannot be digested by the body and passes through unchanged. It is found in cereal-based foods such as wholemeal bread, wholewheat pasta, brown rice, wholewheat and bran breakfast cereals and the skins of some fruits and vegetables.

Both soluble and insoluble fibre are important to maintain a healthy digestive system. Low intakes of dietary fibre are associated with an increased risk of bowel disease as well as disorders such as constipation. Fibre, particularly cereal (insoluble) fibre, helps to regulate bowel function and prevent intestinal disorders such as piles (haemorrhoids) and diverticular disease.

Dietary fibre is also thought to offer some protection against diseases such as large bowel cancer, and is sometimes successful in treating irritable bowel syndrome. Research suggests that small amounts of soluble fibre are digested into the bloodstream and this is thought to help to lower high cholesterol levels in the blood. It is believed that fibre reduces the rate at which carbohydrates are digested and transformed into blood sugar, a fact which has implications for diabetics.

It is very important to drink plenty of non-alcoholic fluids as part of a healthy diet – at least eight glasses a day (preferably water). This is especially true when the diet is high in fibre. Undigested fibre absorbs and holds fluid in the gut to form soft and bulky stools which move quickly and efficiently along the bowel. As already stated, water is the best beverage, but some fruit juices, milk (low-fat in the case of adults) and limited amounts of coffee and tea are all acceptable. If insufficient liquid is drunk, constipation may be the result.

Left: Increase your fibre intake at breakfast time by enjoying high fibre muesli sprinkled over fresh fruit. The tastiest and healthiest muesli is home-made from oats, bran flakes, wheatgerm, dried fruit, nuts and seeds.

INTRODUCING MORE FIBRE

There are many simple ways of introducing fibre into your diet. Some years ago, it became fashionable to boost fibre by simply sprinkling bran on anything and everything, from breakfast cereals to stews and desserts. While wheat bran is a good source of fibre, simply adding it to your food is no substitute for getting fibre from food itself. Wheat bran can be an irritant; it is high in substances called phytates, which can interfere with the absorption of essential minerals such as iron, calcium and zinc.

It is important to obtain a mixture of both soluble and insoluble fibre from a variety of foods that are naturally good sources of fibre, rather than taking supplements. By choosing foods that are naturally high in fibre you will benefit from other important nutrients such as vitamins and minerals in those foods. For example, switching from white bread, pasta and rice to wholemeal or wholegrain alternatives is an easy way of introducing more fibre into your diet, as is choosing a wholewheat breakfast cereal or serving a jacket potato with a meal.

Many foods that are higher in fibre also tend to be filling, bulky and relatively low in calories. Weight-watchers and slimmers who fill up on high fibre, starchy foods like wholegrain cereals, bread, pasta and rice have less room for refined foods which tend to be higher in fat and sugar.

Nowadays, many packaged foods are labelled with nutritional information, including the dietary fibre content. It is a good idea to get into the habit of reading the labels, not just for the amount of fibre, but also for the levels of other nutrients. Food charts, listing the fibre content of everyday foods, are included in this book.

Right: Wholemeal bread is a good source of fibre, and is full of flavour. It is available in a wide range, from the traditional farmhouse loaf to rolls, muffins and pitta bread.

FIBRE BOOSTERS

Quick and easy ways of increasing the amount of fibre in the diet:
• Choose wholemeal, wholegrain, high fibre, brown or granary bread for snacks, sandwiches and serving with meals. Look out for wholemeal pitta bread, rolls, muffins, scones, buns, biscuits, crackers and crispbreads, too. Add wholemeal breadcrumbs to stuffings, coatings and toppings.
• Choose wholemeal flour rather than white flour, and wholemeal pasta instead of white pasta.
• Brown rice has more fibre than white rice and has a delicious, nutty taste. Try a medley of brown and wild rice.
• Select wholewheat breakfast cereals which are naturally high in fibre rather than adding neat bran to cereals. Make your own high fibre muesli by mixing oats, bran flakes, wheatgerm, dried fruit, nuts and seeds. Serve topped with some fresh fruit.
• Use wholewheat breakfast cereals and muesli in baking, for topping fruit crumble, as coatings, in cheesecake bases, meatloaves and burgers.
• Base a main course entirely on pulses rather than meat or fish; alternatively, replace some of the meat with cooked beans or lentils. Soups can be similarly extended and fresh vegetables, such as carrots and potatoes, can be added.
• Wash, but don't peel fruit and vegetables where possible. When making vegetable soups or sauces, leave the vegetables in chunks. If you must purée them, do not sieve the purée or you will lose much of the valuable fibre.
• Add grated root vegetables, such as potatoes or parsnips, to casseroles, lasagne, cottage pie and stews.
• Enjoy at least five portions of fresh vegetables or fruit every day, on their own or in salads, lightly cooked or, ideally, raw.
• Snack on dried fruit, or use it in cakes, scones, rock cakes and muffins. Dried fruit salad is delicious.

STORECUPBOARD INGREDIENTS

Many simple, high fibre ingredients are available in packets or cans. Keep your pantry or storecupboard stocked with the items in the list that follows and increasing the fibre content of a snack or meal will always be easy.

BREAKFAST CEREALS

A wide variety of breakfast cereals is available. Wholewheat or wholegrain varieties are the best choice for fibre – preferably those that are also low in fat and sugar. Try using wholewheat breakfast cereals when making home-made bakes such as muesli bars and flapjacks, for crumble toppings and cheesecake bases, for coating foods, in tealoaves and meatloaves or burgers.

BROWN RICE

There are many varieties of brown rice available including long grain, basmati, jasmine and risotto, as well as canned brown rice and boil-in-the-bag brown rice for convenience.

The flavour of brown rice is quite nutty, and because the rice undergoes only minor milling, the bran layer is retained, making it higher in fibre, vitamins and minerals than white rice. Rice is also low in fat. Cooking time for brown rice is about 35 minutes, during which time it expands and increases by up to three times the volume. Allow at least 50g/2oz/ 1/3 cup uncooked rice per person.

CANNED BEANS AND OTHER PULSES

There are many kinds of canned pulses, such as beans, peas and lentils, available in shops and supermarkets. They include black-eyed beans, butter beans, pinto beans, chick-peas, flageolet beans, lentils, peas and red kidney beans. They are low in fat and high in protein, vitamins and minerals.

Add beans and other pulses to dishes such as salads, soups, pâtés and burgers or try mashing cooked pulses to use as a basis for dips, served with vegetable crudités.

DRIED BEANS AND OTHER PULSES

Dried pulses are very useful storecupboard items. When buying, choose dried pulses that are plump, bright and clear in colour. Store in an airtight container and use within one year.

Many dried pulses need to be soaked in water before being cooked and should be boiled for a period, until tender. The older the beans are, the longer they will take to cook. Salt should be added only at the end of the cooking time; if added sooner, it will toughen the beans. Some beans, such as red kidney beans, contain a toxic substance known as haemaglutinin which can lead to acute gastroenteritis if it is not destroyed by adequate cooking. These beans need to be boiled vigorously for at least 10 minutes to destroy the haemaglutinin, then simmered until they are tender.

DRIED FRUIT

Supermarkets, health-food stores and even corner shops stock a good selection of dried fruit and ready-to-eat dried fruit including apples, apricots, bananas, currants, figs, kiwi fruit, lychees, mangoes, papayas, peaches, pears, pineapple, prunes, raisins and

Left: Dried apricots make a delicious snack between meals and are very high in fibre.

sultanas. They are very versatile and can be used in both sweet and savoury dishes. Add dried fruit to your breakfast cereal, muesli or porridge and use it in cake, scone, biscuit, dessert and muffin recipes.

NUTS

Nuts are a good source of dietary fibre and have many uses in a wide selection of sweet and savoury dishes. They also make a tasty snack, but as they are high in fat and calories, eat them only in small quantities. Nuts yielding generous amounts of dietary fibre include almonds, brazil nuts, hazelnuts, peanuts, pecan nuts, pistachios and walnuts.

Some nuts, such as almonds and hazelnuts, are also a good source of vitamin E. Add nuts to salads, cakes and bakes, biscuits, desserts, stuffings, coatings and stir-fries. Nuts also make a good topping for a gratin and can be used as a garnish for savoury dishes or a decoration for desserts.

OATS AND OATMEAL

Oats and oatmeal are valuable sources of soluble fibre which is absorbed into the body and is thought to help reduce high levels of blood cholesterol. Oats and oatmeal come in a variety of forms including porridge oats, quick-cook oats, jumbo oats, fine and medium oatmeal. Use oats in muesli and oatcakes, mixed with flour for breads and rolls, cakes and bakes, such as gingerbread and flapjacks, and crumble toppings. Fine oatmeal also makes a good thickener for soups and sauces.

SEEDS

Seeds such as sesame, sunflower and pumpkin are all good sources of dietary fibre. They can be eaten on their own as a snack or added to dishes such as salads, stir-fries, stuffings, cakes and bakes, coatings, muesli, biscuits and crackers. Seeds also contain vitamins and minerals but are high in fat and calories, so should be eaten in small quantities.

SPICES

Spices are invaluable items for the storecupboard; they can enhance and transform everyday dishes. Keep them in airtight, tinted-glass containers in a cool, dark cupboard. Ground spices should be used within six months and whole spices within a year, so it is wise to buy them in small quantities. Freshly ground spices provide the best flavour and aroma, so it is well worth investing in a small pestle and mortar so that you can grind your own.

SUGARS AND HONEY

There is no calorific difference between white (refined) and brown (unrefined) sugar but the flavours vary. Many of the recipes in this book use soft light brown sugar but other sugars, such as caster or dark muscovado, can be used instead.

Honey is also used in sweet and savoury dishes and clear honey is specified in most recipes. Honey is a little sweeter than sugar, so if you are substituting it for sugar you will probably need slightly less.

WHEAT BRAN

Natural wheat bran is the hard outer layer or casing that surrounds the wheat grain. It is high in fibre. Other brans such as rice bran, oat bran and soya bran are also available but wheat bran is the most common.

Bran is a useful ingredient and can be added to breads, muffins and cereals, but sprinkling bran on a dish is no substitute for getting fibre from food.

WHOLEMEAL BISCUITS AND CRACKERS

Wholemeal or wholewheat biscuits and high fibre crackers make good storecupboard standbys for a healthy, high fibre snack. Serve savoury varieties with a selection of cheeses, or spread with butter or a low-fat spread. Crushed, sweet wholemeal biscuits are good for cheesecake bases and crunchy toppings for fruity desserts.

WHOLEMEAL FLOUR

Wholemeal or wholewheat flour is 100 per cent flour that has been milled from the whole of the wheat grain. "Whole" means that the grain has not had the bran, vitamins and minerals refined out – in other words it has had nothing added or removed, so it contains all the original nutrients and is by far the healthiest option.

Wholemeal flour is coarser than white flour and is available in several forms including plain, self-raising and strong. It is very versatile and can be used in many dishes that traditionally specify white flour, including cakes, bakes, breads, pastry, biscuits and crackers. It makes a good thickener for sauces and can be used to coat foods. A mixture of half wholemeal and half white flour can be used in recipes where a lighter flour is required.

Above: It is always worth keeping a useful selection of basic items in your storecupboard, including dried as well as canned ingredients.

WHOLEWHEAT PASTA

Dried wholewheat or wholemeal pasta is a good source of dietary fibre and carbohydrate. It is also low in fat and contains some B vitamins. It is an essential storecupboard item and is a great basis for many quick and easy, nutritious meals. Pasta is very versatile and can be used in many dishes including salads, pasta bakes and filled pasta, which can be topped with low-fat sauces. Allow 115–225g/4–8oz/1–2 cups pasta per serving for a main course and 50–115g/2–4oz/1/2–1 cup per person for a starter. Dried wholewheat pasta cooks in about 12 minutes.

FRESH FOODS AND INGREDIENTS

Fresh vegetables and fruit play a vitally important part in a high fibre diet. They are particularly wholesome if eaten raw and unpeeled, where this is possible. Wholemeal bread and bakes are also excellent sources of fibre, as well as wholemeal pastas and rice.

FRESH BEANS AND OTHER LEGUMES

There are many varieties of fresh beans and legumes available, including peas, broad beans and runner beans and more unusual ones such as fresh flageolet beans and butter beans. Fresh corn on the cob and baby sweetcorn are also popular.

All are good sources of dietary fibre and contain other nutrients including vitamins and minerals. Beans and legumes (known as pulses when dried) are very versatile and can be used in many dishes including salads, stir-fries, casseroles, pasta sauces, soups and curries. Some varieties, such as sugar-snap peas and mangetouts, can be eaten either raw or cooked.

FRESH FRUIT

Fresh fruit plays an important part in a healthy, balanced, high fibre diet. Choose fruits that contain useful amounts of fibre such as apples, pears, bananas, oranges and peaches, or berries such as raspberries, blackberries and gooseberries, not forgetting some more exotic fruits, including guavas and mangoes.

Fruits are very versatile and can be enjoyed raw or cooked, on their own or as part of a recipe. They are also good sources of vitamins and minerals. Avoid peeling them, where possible, for maximum goodness.

FRESH HERBS

In cookery, herbs are used mainly for their flavouring and seasoning properties, as well as for adding colour and texture. Simply adding a single herb or a combination of herbs can transform everyday dishes into delicious meals. Herbs are also very low in fat and calories and some, such as parsley, provide a useful balance of vitamins and minerals.

FRESH VEGETABLES

Fresh vegetables, like fresh fruit, play an important part in a healthy, balanced diet. We are advised to eat at least five portions of fruit and vegetables each day. Vegetables are nutritious and are valuable sources of vitamins and minerals, some being especially rich in vitamins A, C and E. Vegetables also contain some dietary fibre and those that are particularly good sources include broccoli, Brussels sprouts, cabbage, carrots, fennel, okra, parsnips, spinach and sweetcorn.

POTATOES

Potatoes are among the most commonly eaten vegetables in the world and are valuable in terms of nutrition. They are high in carbohydrate, low in fat and contain some vitamin C and dietary fibre. Potatoes contain more dietary fibre when eaten unpeeled. Wash old and new potatoes thoroughly and cook them with their skins on – baked, boiled or roasted. Try mashed potatoes (with their skins left on, of course!) as a topping on pies and bakes. Use skimmed milk, fromage frais, reduced-fat hard cheese or herbs to add flavour. For roast potatoes use only a small amount of oil, and if you must make chips, leave the skins on and cut the chips thickly, using a knife.

WHOLEMEAL BAKES AND BREAD

Bakes such as wholemeal pitta breads, scones, muffins and teacakes make good, high fibre snacks or treats. Choose wholemeal or wholegrain varieties whenever possible.

Bread is available in many varieties and is a good source of carbohydrate as well as being low in fat. It also contains some calcium, iron and B vitamins and wholemeal varieties are high in fibre.

Left: Eat fresh fruit regularly as it contains vitamin C as well as being high in fibre.

HIGH FIBRE MEAL PLANNER

In the at-a-glance guide that follows, six typical sweet and savoury dishes are contrasted with similar dishes that have been altered slightly to increase their fibre content (the full recipes are given in this book). The changes are simple, but the results are significant. Each dish has been analysed to reveal the dietary fibre content of a typical serving, and to illustrate how easy it is to boost your intake of fibre by making only minimal changes to your diet. This will help you to choose the right ingredients when you prepare your own recipes.

FRESH TOMATO SOUP *VERSUS* FRESH TOMATO, LENTIL AND ONION SOUP

The dietary fibre content of an average portion of fresh tomato soup is 3.09g. Use fewer tomatoes and add onions and lentils, however, and the dietary fibre content per portion rises a little to 4.27g.

CHEESE AND TOMATO PIZZA WITH WHITE SCONE BASE *VERSUS* COURGETTE, SWEETCORN AND PLUM TOMATO PIZZA WITH WHOLEMEAL BASE

With a white scone base, an average slice of cheese and tomato pizza has a dietary fibre content of 1.99g. Use wholemeal flour for the base and add mushrooms, courgettes, onion and sweetcorn to the topping, and the dietary fibre content rises to 4.93g.

WHITE PASTA SALAD WITH PEPPERS AND MUSHROOMS *VERSUS* ROAST PEPPER AND WILD MUSHROOM PASTA SALAD

The dietary fibre content of an average portion of pasta salad with peppers and mushrooms is 5.82g. To boost this to 9.37g, use wholemeal pasta instead of white pasta and sultanas instead of cherry tomatoes.

HOME-MADE COLESLAW *VERSUS* CARROT, RAISIN AND APRICOT COLESLAW

An average portion of home-made coleslaw has a dietary fibre content of 2.92g. If the quantity of cabbage is reduced slightly and celery, raisins and ready-to-eat dried apricots are added, this rises to 4.25g.

APPLE CRUMBLE MADE USING WHITE FLOUR *VERSUS* PEACH AND RASPBERRY CRUMBLE

The dietary fibre content of an average portion of apple crumble is 3.86g. However, if a mixture of wholemeal flour and oatmeal is used in place of white flour to make the crumble topping, and peaches and raspberries replace apples for the base, this will rise to 5.22g.

HIGH FIBRE FOOD CHARTS

The following tables are an at-a-glance guide to the dietary fibre content of a range of commonly eaten foods. The figures show the amount of fibre per 100g/3¾oz, unless otherwise stated. For cereals, a 30g/1¾oz serving size is also given.

BEANS, PEAS AND LENTILS	FIBRE (G)
baked beans in tomato sauce	3.7
broad beans, boiled	6.5
butter beans, canned	4.6
chick-peas, canned	4.1
green beans, boiled	4.1
lentils, brown and green, boiled	3.8
lentils, red split, boiled	1.9
mangetout peas, boiled	2.2
peas, boiled	5.1
red kidney beans, canned	6.2
runner beans, boiled	1.9

BISCUITS	FIBRE (G)
cream cracker	2.2
cream cracker (each)	0.2
crispbread, rye	11.7
crispbread, rye (each)	1.2
crispbread, high fibre	17.9
crispbread, high fibre (each)	1.8
digestive, plain	2.2
digestive, plain (each)	0.3
oatcake	5.9
oatcake (each)	0.8
shortbread finger	1.9
shortbread finger (each)	0.2

BREADS	FIBRE (G)
brown bread	3.5
brown bread (1 medium slice)	1.3
granary bread	4.3
granary bread (1 medium slice)	1.5
white pitta bread	2.2
white pitta bread (1 medium pitta)	1.4
wholemeal pitta bread	6.4
wholemeal pitta (1 medium pitta)	4.1
rye bread	4.4
rye bread (1 average slice)	1.1
white bread	1.5
white bread (1 medium slice)	0.5
white bread with added fibre	3.1
white bread with added fibre (1 medium slice)	1.1
wholemeal bread	5.8
wholemeal bread (1 medium slice)	2.1

The information presented in these tables has been compiled from McCance and Widdowson's *The Composition of Foods*, 5th edition and relevant supplements. Data are reproduced with the kind permission of the Royal Society of Chemistry and the Controller of Her Majesty's Stationery Office.

BREAKFAST CEREALS	FIBRE (G)
All-bran	24.5
All-bran (30g serving)	7.4
Branflakes	13.0
Branflakes (30g serving)	3.9
Cornflakes	0.9
Cornflakes (30g serving)	0.3
Frosties	0.6
Frosties (30g serving)	0.2
Fruit 'n' fibre	7.0
Fruit 'n' fibre (30g serving)	2.1
muesli – Swiss style	6.4
muesli – Swiss style (30g serving)	1.9
muesli – no added sugar	7.6
muesli – no added sugar (30g)	2.3
porridge	0.8
porridge (30g serving)	0.2
Puffed Wheat	5.6
Puffed Wheat (30g serving)	1.7
Ready Brek	7.2
Ready Brek (30g serving)	2.2
Rice Crispies	0.7
Rice Crispies (30g serving)	0.2
Shredded Wheat	9.8
Shredded Wheat (30g serving)	2.9
Sultana Bran	10.0
Sultana Bran (30g serving)	3.0
Weetabix	9.7
Weetabix (each)	1.9

Left: Apples and other fresh fruit make a healthy snack at any time of the day. If possible, increase your fibre intake by eating the skins of all fruit with edible skins.

Right: Broccoli or other fresh vegetables should be eaten every day. Consuming them raw rather than cooked is a much more healthy way of eating them.

CAKES AND BAKES	FIBRE (G)
fruit cake, rich	1.7
fruit cake, rich (per slice)	1.2
fruit cake, wholemeal	2.4
fruit cake, wholemeal (per slice)	1.7
sponge cake	0.9
sponge cake (per slice)	0.5
muffin, plain	2.0
muffin, plain (each)	1.4
muffin, bran	7.7
muffin, bran (each)	5.4
scone, plain	1.9
scone, plain (each)	0.9
scone, wholemeal	5.2
scone, wholemeal (each)	2.6

FLOURS AND GRAINS	FIBRE (G)
wheat bran	36.4
oatmeal	6.8
porridge oats	7.0
wheat flour, brown	6.4
wheat flour, white	3.1
wheat flour, wholemeal	9.0
wheatgerm	15.6
brown rice, boiled	0.8
white rice, boiled	0.1
white spaghetti, boiled	1.2
wholemeal spaghetti, boiled	3.5

Left: Sweet potatoes are rich in fibre and vitamins and do not take as long as ordinary potatoes to cook. Scrub them clean and bake in a hot oven in their skins for 10–15 minutes.

FRUIT	FIBRE (G)
(Figures given are for raw fruit unless otherwise stated)	
apple, eating	1.8
apple, eating (each)	1.8
apricots, dried (ready-to-eat)	6.3
avocado	3.4
banana	1.1
banana (each)	1.1
blackberries	3.1
dates, dried	3.4
figs, dried (ready-to-eat)	6.9
gooseberries, stewed, no sugar	2.0
grapefruit	1.3
grapefruit (half)	1.0
guava	3.7
kiwi fruit	1.9
kiwi fruit (each)	1.1
mango	2.6
orange	1.7
orange (each)	2.7
passion fruit	3.3
passion fruit (each)	0.5
peach	1.5
peach (each)	1.7
peaches, dried (ready-to-eat)	7.3
pear	2.2
pear (each)	3.3
pears, dried (ready-to-eat)	8.3
pineapple	1.2
pineapple, dried (ready-to-eat)	8.1
prunes (ready-to-eat)	5.7
raisins	2.0
raspberries	2.5
sultanas	2.0

NUTS AND SEEDS	FIBRE (G)
almonds	7.4
brazil nuts	4.3
chestnuts	4.1
desiccated coconut	13.7
hazelnuts	6.5
peanuts	6.2
pecan nuts	4.7
pistachio nuts	6.1
pumpkin seeds	5.3
sesame seeds	7.9
sunflower seeds	6.0
walnuts	3.5

PASTRY	FIBRE (G)
shortcrust, cooked	2.2
wholemeal shortcrust, cooked	6.3

VEGETABLES	FIBRE (G)
broccoli, boiled	2.3
Brussels sprouts, boiled	3.1
cabbage, raw	2.4
cabbage, boiled	1.8
carrots, raw	2.4
carrots, boiled	2.5
celeriac, boiled	3.2
fennel, boiled	2.3
leeks, boiled	1.7
okra, boiled	3.6
onions, raw	1.4
parsnips, boiled	4.7
potatoes, baked, flesh and skin	2.7
potatoes, boiled	1.2
Quorn (mycoprotein)	4.8
spinach, raw	2.1
spinach, boiled	2.1
spring greens, boiled	2.6
squash, baked	2.1
sweet potatoes, boiled	2.3
sweetcorn kernels, canned	1.4
turnip, boiled	1.9

SOUPS AND STARTERS

For simple soups that are full of fibre, make the most of chick-peas, beans and lentils, alone or with fresh vegetables such as carrots, onions and leeks. Spicy Chick-pea and Bacon Soup is a sure winner or, for vegetarians, go green with the very wholesome Pea, Leek and Broccoli Soup. Starters include a delicious dip with butter beans as the prime ingredient, which is accompanied by crunchy vegetable crudités, while kidney beans combine with fresh mushrooms to make an unforgettable pâté. Vegetables are worthy of a starring role, served on their own as in Vegetables Provençal, or with chicken in a wonderful, warm salad. Serve soups and starters with wholemeal or granary bread to boost the fibre content of your meal still further.

Spicy Chick-pea and Bacon Soup

This is a tasty mixture of chick-peas and bacon flavoured with a subtle mix of spices.

INGREDIENTS

Serves 4–6

10ml/2 tsp sunflower oil
1 onion, chopped
2 garlic cloves, crushed
5ml/1 tsp each garam masala, ground coriander, ground cumin and ground turmeric
2.5ml/½ tsp hot chilli powder
30ml/2 tbsp plain wholemeal flour
600ml/1 pint/2½ cups vegetable stock
400g/14oz can chopped tomatoes
400g/14oz can chick-peas, rinsed and drained
6 rashers lean smoked back bacon
salt and ground black pepper
coriander sprigs, to garnish

1 Heat the oil in a large saucepan. Add the onion and garlic and cook for 5 minutes, stirring occasionally so that the mixture does not burn.

2 Add the spices and flour and cook for 1 minute, stirring.

3 Gradually add the stock, stirring constantly, and then add the tomatoes and chick-peas.

4 Bring to the boil, stirring, then cover and simmer for 25 minutes, stirring occasionally.

5 Meanwhile, grill the bacon for about 2–3 minutes on each side.

6 Dice the grilled bacon, cutting and reserving a few diamond-shaped pieces for garnishing. Stir the diced pieces into the hot soup. Season to taste, reheat gently until piping hot and ladle the soup into bowls. Garnish each bowl with a coriander sprig and the reserved bacon. Serve immediately.

VARIATION

Use other canned beans such as red kidney beans or flageolet beans in place of the chick-peas, for a different flavour.

NUTRITION NOTES

Per portion:	
Energy	207kcals/874kJ
Protein	15.56g
Fat	7.28g
Saturated fat	1.43g
Carbohydrate	22.40g
Fibre	4.82g
Added sugar	0.02g
Sodium	1.17g

Fresh Tomato, Lentil and Onion Soup

This delicious, wholesome soup is ideal served with thick slices of wholemeal or granary bread.

INGREDIENTS

Serves 4–6

10ml/2 tsp sunflower oil
1 large onion, chopped
2 celery sticks, chopped
175g/6oz/¾ cup split red lentils
2 large tomatoes, skinned and
    roughly chopped
900ml/1½ pints/3¾ cups
    vegetable stock
10ml/2 tsp dried *herbes
    de Provence*
salt and ground black pepper
chopped fresh parsley, to garnish

1 Heat the oil in a large saucepan. Add the onion and celery and cook for 5 minutes, stirring occasionally. Add the lentils and cook for 1 minute.

2 Stir in the tomatoes, stock, herbs and seasoning. Cover, bring to the boil and simmer for about 20 minutes, stirring occasionally.

3 When the lentils are cooked and tender, remove the soup from the heat and set aside to cool slightly.

4 Purée in a blender or food processor until smooth. Adjust the seasoning, return to the saucepan and reheat gently until piping hot. Ladle into soup bowls and garnish each with chopped parsley.

NUTRITION NOTES

Per portion:

Energy	202kcals/856kJ
Protein	12.40g
Fat	3.07g
Saturated fat	0.38g
Carbohydrate	33.34g
Fibre	4.27g
Added sugar	0.04g
Sodium	0.54g

Pea, Leek and Broccoli Soup

A nutritious soup, full of flavour and perfect for warming those chilly winter evenings.

INGREDIENTS

Serves 4–6

1 onion, chopped
225g/8oz/2 cups leeks
    (trimmed weight), sliced
225g/8oz unpeeled potatoes, diced
900ml/1½ pints/3¾ cups
    vegetable stock
1 bay leaf
225g/8oz broccoli florets
175g/6oz/1½ cups frozen peas
30–45ml/2–3 tbsp chopped
    fresh parsley
salt and ground black pepper
parsley leaves, to garnish

1 Put the onion, leeks, potatoes, stock and bay leaf in a large saucepan and mix together. Cover, bring to the boil and simmer for 10 minutes, stirring.

2 Add the broccoli and peas, cover, return to the boil and simmer for a further 10 minutes, stirring from time to time.

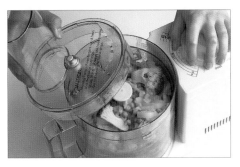

3 Leave to cool slightly and remove and discard the bay leaf. Purée in a blender or food processor until smooth.

COOK'S TIP

If you prefer, cut the vegetables finely and leave the cooked soup chunky rather than puréeing it.

4 Add the chopped fresh parsley, season to taste and process again briefly. Return the soup to the saucepan and reheat gently until piping hot. Ladle into soup bowls and garnish with parsley leaves.

--- NUTRITION NOTES ---

Per portion:

Energy	125kcals/528kJ
Protein	8.11g
Fat	1.92g
Saturated fat	0.26g
Carbohydrate	19.94g
Fibre	6.31g
Added sugar	0.04g
Sodium	0.52g

Curried Celery Soup

A successful combination of flavours, this warming soup is excellent served with warm wholemeal bread rolls or wholemeal pitta bread.

INGREDIENTS

Serves 4–6

10ml/2 tsp olive oil
1 onion, chopped
1 leek, washed and sliced
675g/1½ lb celery, chopped
15ml/1 tbsp medium or hot
  curry powder
225g/8oz unpeeled potatoes,
  washed and diced
900ml/1½ pints/3¾ cups
  vegetable stock
1 bouquet garni
30ml/2 tbsp chopped fresh
  mixed herbs
salt and ground black pepper
celery seeds and leaves, to garnish

1 Heat the oil in a large saucepan. Add the onion, leek and celery, cover and cook gently for 10 minutes, stirring occasionally.

2 Add the curry powder and cook for 2 minutes, stirring occasionally.

3 Add the potatoes, stock and bouquet garni, cover, and bring to the boil. Simmer for 20 minutes, until the vegetables are tender.

4 Remove the saucepan from the heat and discard the bouquet garni. Set the soup aside and allow it to cool slightly.

5 Purée the soup in a blender or food processor until smooth.

6 Add the chopped fresh mixed herbs, season to taste and process again briefly. Return the soup to the saucepan and reheat gently until piping hot. Ladle into soup bowls and garnish each with a sprinkling of celery seeds and some celery leaves.

VARIATION

For a tasty and sweeter change, use celeriac and sweet potatoes in place of celery and standard potatoes.

NUTRITION NOTES

Per portion:

Energy	102kcals/431kJ
Protein	3.72g
Fat	2.93g
Saturated fat	0.25g
Carbohydrate	16.11g
Fibre	4.44g
Added sugar	0.04g
Sodium	0.62g

Mushroom and Bean Pâté

Serve this unusual vegetarian pâté with wholemeal bread or toast for a starter or a light suppertime snack. It also has the benefit of being very low in fat.

INGREDIENTS

Serves 12

450g/1 lb/6 cups mushrooms, sliced
1 onion, chopped
2 garlic cloves, crushed
1 red pepper, seeded and diced
30ml/2 tbsp vegetable stock
30ml/2 tbsp dry white wine
400g/14oz can red kidney beans,
   rinsed and drained
1 egg, beaten
50g/2oz/1 cup fresh
   wholemeal breadcrumbs
15ml/1 tbsp chopped fresh thyme
15ml/1 tbsp chopped
   fresh rosemary
salt and ground black pepper
lettuce and cherry tomatoes, to garnish

1 Preheat the oven to 180°C/350°F/ Gas 4. Lightly grease and line a non-stick 900g/2 lb loaf tin. Put the mushrooms, onion, garlic, red pepper, stock and wine in a saucepan. Cover and cook for 10 minutes. Stir a little.

2 Set aside to cool slightly, then purée the mixture with the kidney beans in a blender or food processor until smooth.

3 Transfer the mixture to a bowl, add the egg, breadcrumbs and herbs and mix thoroughly. Season to taste.

4 Spoon into the prepared tin and level the surface. Bake for about 45–60 minutes, until lightly set and browned on top. Place on a wire rack and allow the pâté to cool completely in the tin. Once cool, cover and refrigerate for several hours. Turn out of the tin and serve in slices. Garnish with lettuce and cherry tomatoes.

NUTRITION NOTES	
Per portion:	
Energy	53kcals/225kJ
Protein	3.42g
Fat	1.04g
Saturated fat	0.26g
Carbohydrate	7.65g
Fibre	2.33g
Added sugar	0.00g
Sodium	0.11g

Butter Bean, Watercress and Herb Dip

A refreshing dip that is especially good served with fresh vegetable crudités and breadsticks or even wholemeal pitta.

INGREDIENTS

Serves 4–6

225g/8oz/1 cup plain
   cottage cheese
400g/14oz can butter beans, rinsed
   and drained
1 bunch spring onions, chopped
50g/2oz watercress, chopped
60ml/4 tbsp reduced-calorie
   mayonnaise
45ml/3 tbsp chopped fresh
   mixed herbs
salt and ground black pepper
watercress sprigs, to garnish
vegetable crudités and breadsticks,
   to serve

1 Put the cottage cheese, butter beans, spring onions, watercress, mayonnaise and herbs in a blender or food processor and blend together until almost smooth.

2 Add seasoning and spoon the mixture carefully into a bowl. Stir well.

3 Cover and chill for several hours before serving.

4 Transfer to a serving dish (or individual dishes) and garnish with watercress sprigs. Serve with vegetable crudités and breadsticks.

--- NUTRITION NOTES ---

Per portion:

Energy	155kcals/650kJ
Protein	12.45g
Fat	6.98g
Saturated fat	2.04g
Carbohydrate	11.25g
Fibre	3.49g
Added sugar	0.38g
Sodium	0.63g

--- VARIATION ---

Try using other canned pulses such as cannellini beans or chick-peas in place of the butter beans.

Vegetables Provençal

The sunshine flavours of the Mediterranean are created in this delicious vegetable dish, ideal for a starter or lunchtime snack, served with fresh, crusty wholemeal bread. It is an excellent dish for vegetarians.

INGREDIENTS

Serves 6
1 onion, sliced
2 leeks, sliced
2 garlic cloves, crushed
1 red pepper, seeded and sliced
1 green pepper, seeded and sliced
1 yellow pepper, seeded and sliced
350g/12oz courgettes, sliced
225g/8oz/3 cups mushrooms, sliced
400g/14oz can chopped tomatoes
30ml/2 tbsp ruby port
30ml/2 tbsp tomato purée
15ml/1 tbsp tomato ketchup
400g/14oz can chick-peas
115g/4oz/1 cup stoned black olives
45ml/3 tbsp chopped fresh
   mixed herbs
salt and ground black pepper
chopped fresh mixed herbs,
   to garnish

1 Put the onion, leeks, garlic, peppers, courgettes and mushrooms into a large saucepan.

2 Add the chopped tomatoes, port, tomato purée and tomato ketchup, and mix well.

3 Rinse and drain the chick-peas and add to the pan.

4 Cover, bring to the boil and simmer gently for 20–30 minutes, until the vegetables are cooked and tender but not overcooked. Stir carefully from time to time.

5 Remove the lid and increase the heat slightly for the last 10 minutes of the cooking time, to thicken the sauce, if liked.

6 Stir in the black olives, chopped fresh mixed herbs and seasoning. Serve the vegetables either hot or cold, garnished with additional chopped fresh mixed herbs.

--- NUTRITION NOTES ---

Per portion:	
Energy	155kcals/654kJ
Protein	8.26g
Fat	4.56g
Saturated fat	0.67g
Carbohydrate	20.19g
Fibre	6.98g
Added sugar	0.52g
Sodium	0.62g

Warm Chicken Salad with Shallots and Mangetouts

Succulent cooked chicken pieces are combined with vegetables in a light chilli dressing.

INGREDIENTS

Serves 6

50g/2oz mixed salad leaves
50g/2oz baby spinach leaves
50g/2oz watercress
30ml/2 tbsp chilli sauce
30ml/2 tbsp dry sherry
15ml/1 tbsp light soy sauce
15ml/1 tbsp tomato ketchup
10ml/2 tsp olive oil
8 shallots, finely chopped
1 garlic clove, crushed
350g/12oz skinless, boneless
    chicken breast, cut into thin strips
1 red pepper, seeded and sliced
175g/6oz mangetouts, trimmed
400g/14oz can baby sweetcorn,
    drained and halved
275g/10oz can brown rice
salt and ground black pepper
parsley sprig, to garnish

1 Arrange the mixed salad leaves, tearing up any large ones, and the spinach leaves on a serving dish. Add the watercress and toss to mix.

2 In a small bowl, mix together the chilli sauce, sherry, soy sauce and tomato ketchup, and set aside.

3 Heat the oil in a large, non-stick frying pan or wok. Add the shallots and garlic and stir-fry over a medium heat for 1 minute.

4 Add the sliced chicken breast to the pan and stir-fry for a further 4–5 minutes, until the chicken pieces are nearly cooked.

5 Add the red pepper, mangetouts, sweetcorn and rice, and stir-fry for 2–3 minutes.

6 Pour in the chilli sauce mixture and stir-fry for 2–3 minutes until hot and bubbling. Season to taste. Spoon the chicken mixture over the salad leaves, toss together to mix and serve immediately, garnished with a sprig of parsley.

VARIATION

Use other kinds of lean meat – such as turkey breast or rindless bacon – in place of the chicken breast.

NUTRITION NOTES

Per portion:

Energy	188kcals/795kJ
Protein	19.22g
Fat	2.81g
Saturated fat	0.52g
Carbohydrate	21.39g
Fibre	3.07g
Added sugar	0.71g
Sodium	1.07g

MEAT, FISH AND POULTRY DISHES

Increasing the fibre content of a meat, fish or poultry dish is simplicity itself. All you need to do is add plenty of vegetables, which will also improve the colour, texture and flavour, or mix the meat with grains, pulses or pasta. This not only serves as a cost-cutting exercise, making the main ingredient go further, but also adds interest, as when couscous is combined with lamb in a spicy stew, or green beans and pasta twists are partnered with smoked bacon to make a salad. For a simple supper, toss mackerel in oatmeal and herbs, grill it until tender and serve with tomatoes, mangetouts and a jacket potato, or make a quick stir-fry using pieces of pork and vegetable chunks.

Pork and Vegetable Stir-fry

A quick and easy stir-fry of pork and vegetables.

INGREDIENTS

Serves 4

225g/8oz can pineapple chunks
15ml/1 tbsp cornflour
30ml/2 tbsp light soy sauce
15ml/1 tbsp each dry sherry,
   soft brown sugar and wine vinegar
5ml/1 tsp five-spice powder
2.5cm/1in piece fresh root ginger
350g/12oz lean pork tenderloin
10ml/2 tsp olive oil
1 red onion, sliced
1 garlic clove, crushed
1 fresh seeded red chilli, chopped
175g/6oz carrots
1 red pepper, seeded and sliced
175g/6oz mangetouts
115g/4oz/½ cup beansprouts
200g/7oz can sweetcorn kernels
30ml/2 tbsp chopped fresh coriander
salt and ground black pepper
15ml/1 tbsp toasted sesame seeds,
   to garnish

1 Drain the pineapple, reserving the juice. In a small bowl, blend the cornflour with the pineapple juice. Add the soy sauce, sherry, sugar, vinegar and spice. Stir to mix and set aside.

2 Peel and finely chop the piece of fresh root ginger. Cut the pork into thin strips. Heat the oil in a large, non-stick frying pan or wok. Add the onion, garlic, chilli and ginger, and stir-fry for 30 seconds. Then add the sliced pork and stir-fry for a 2–3 minutes.

3 Cut the carrots into matchstick strips. Add to the wok with the red pepper and stir-fry for 2–3 minutes. Add the mangetouts, beansprouts and the drained sweetcorn, and stir-fry for 1–2 minutes.

4 Pour in the sauce mixture and the reserved pineapple and stir-fry until the sauce thickens. Reduce the heat and stir-fry for a further 1–2 minutes. Stir in the coriander and season to taste. Sprinkle with sesame seeds and serve immediately.

— NUTRITION NOTES —	
Per portion:	
Energy	327kcals/1380kJ
Protein	24.95g
Fat	7.90g
Saturated fat	1.89g
Carbohydrate	40.81g
Fibre	4.77g
Added sugar	5.38g
Sodium	0.73g

Lamb with Vegetables

A good variety of vegetables makes this a healthy dish.

INGREDIENTS

Serves 6

juice of 1 lemon
15ml/1 tbsp soy sauce
15ml/1 tbsp dry sherry
1 garlic clove, crushed
10ml/2 tsp chopped fresh rosemary
6 lean chump or loin lamb chops
1 red onion, cut into 8 pieces
1 onion, cut into 8 pieces
1 red, 1 yellow and 1 green pepper,
    seeded and cut into chunks
4 courgettes, thickly sliced
350g/12oz/4½ cups button mushrooms
30ml/2 tbsp olive oil
4 plum tomatoes, peeled
400g/14oz can baby sweetcorn
60ml/4 tbsp chopped fresh basil
15–30ml/1–2 tbsp balsamic vinegar
salt and ground black pepper
basil sprigs, to garnish
jacket potatoes, to serve

1 In a shallow dish, mix together the lemon juice, soy sauce, sherry, garlic and rosemary. Coat the lamb chops in the marinade. Cover and refrigerate for 2 hours.

2 Preheat the oven to 200°C/400°F/ Gas 6. Put the onions, peppers, courgettes and mushrooms in a roasting tin, drizzle over the oil and toss the vegetables. Bake for 25 minutes.

NUTRITION NOTES

Per portion:

Energy	273kcals/1143kJ
Protein	26.95g
Fat	12.60g
Saturated fat	4.22g
Carbohydrate	13.15g
Fibre	4.99g
Added sugar	0.10g
Sodium	0.91g

3 Quarter the tomatoes and stir in with the sweetcorn. Bake for a further 10 minutes, until all the vegetables are just tender and slightly browned at the edges. Then add the chopped fresh basil, sprinkle over the balsamic vinegar and season to taste, stirring thoroughly to mix well.

4 Preheat the grill. Place the lamb chops under a medium grill for about 6 minutes on each side until cooked, turning over once. Brush the chops with any remaining marinade while they are cooking, to prevent them drying out. Place the chops on individual serving plates with the vegetables, garnish with basil sprigs and serve with jacket potatoes.

Spiced Lamb and Vegetable Couscous

A delicious stew of tender lamb and vegetables, served with plenty of couscous.

INGREDIENTS

Serves 6

350g/12oz lean lamb fillet, cut into 2cm/¾in cubes
30ml/2 tbsp wholemeal plain flour, seasoned
10ml/2 tsp sunflower oil
1 onion, chopped
2 garlic cloves, crushed
1 red pepper, seeded and diced
5ml/1 tsp ground coriander
5ml/1 tsp ground cumin
5ml/1 tsp ground allspice
2.5ml/½ tsp hot chilli powder
300ml/½ pint/1¼ cups lamb stock
400g/14oz can chopped tomatoes
225g/8oz carrots, sliced
175g/6oz parsnips, sliced
175g/6oz courgettes, sliced
175g/6oz/2½ cups closed cup mushrooms, quartered
225g/8oz frozen broad beans
115g/4oz/¾ cup sultanas
450g/1 lb/2¾ cups quick-cook couscous
salt and ground black pepper
fresh coriander, to garnish

1 Toss the lamb fillet in the seasoned flour. Heat the oil in a large saucepan and add the lamb, onion, garlic and pepper. Cook for 5 minutes, stirring frequently.

2 Add any remaining flour and the spices and cook for 1 minute, stirring continuously.

3 Gradually add the stock, continuing to stir, then add the tomatoes, carrots and parsnips, and mix well.

4 Bring to the boil, stirring, then cover and simmer for 30 minutes, stirring occasionally.

5 Add the courgettes, mushrooms, broad beans and sultanas. Cover, return to the boil and simmer for a further 20–30 minutes, until the lamb and vegetables are tender, stirring occasionally. Season to taste.

6 Meanwhile, soak the couscous and steam in a colander lined with a tea towel over a pan of boiling water for 20 minutes, until cooked, or according to the packet instructions. Pile the cooked couscous on to a warmed serving platter or individual plates and top with the lamb and vegetable stew. Garnish with fresh coriander and serve immediately.

NUTRITION NOTES

Per portion:

Energy	439kcals/1846kJ
Protein	23.29g
Fat	8.15g
Saturated fat	2.57g
Carbohydrate	72.98g
Fibre	7.34g
Added sugar	0.00g
Sodium	0.18g

VARIATION

As a tasty alternative to couscous, you might prefer to serve this lamb and vegetable stew on a bed of cooked bulgur wheat or brown rice.

Chicken and Bean Risotto

Brown rice, red kidney beans, sweetcorn and broccoli all add extra fibre to this risotto.

INGREDIENTS

Serves 4–6

1 onion, chopped
2 garlic cloves, crushed
1 fresh red chilli, seeded and
   finely chopped
175g/6oz/2¼ cups
   mushrooms, sliced
2 celery sticks, chopped
225g/8oz/1 cup long grain brown rice
450ml/¾ pint/scant 2 cups stock
150ml/¼ pint/⅔ cup white wine
400g/14oz can red kidney beans
225g/8oz skinless, boneless chicken
   breast, diced
200g/7oz can sweetcorn kernels
115g/4oz/¾ cup sultanas
175g/6oz small broccoli florets
30–45ml/2–3 tbsp chopped fresh
   mixed herbs
salt and ground black pepper

1 Put the onion, garlic, chilli, mushrooms, celery, rice, stock and wine in a saucepan. Cover, bring to the boil and simmer for 15 minutes.

2 Rinse and drain the kidney beans. Stir the chicken, kidney beans, sweetcorn and sultanas into the pan. Cook for a further 20 minutes, until almost all the liquid has been absorbed.

3 Cook the broccoli in boiling water for 5 minutes, then drain.

--- COOK'S TIP ---

When preparing fresh chillies, wear gloves to protect your hands or wash your hands well afterwards and avoid touching your eyes. Use 5ml/1 tsp hot chilli powder in place of the fresh chilli, if you like.

4 Stir the broccoli and chopped herbs into the risotto, season to taste and serve immediately.

--- NUTRITION NOTES ---

Per portion:	
Energy	563kcals/2383kJ
Protein	31.01g
Fat	5.73g
Saturated fat	1.31g
Carbohydrate	96.85g
Fibre	8.72g
Added sugar	0.02g
Sodium	0.66g

Smoked Bacon and Green Bean Pasta Salad

A tasty pasta salad subtly flavoured with smoked bacon and tossed together in a light, flavoursome dressing.

INGREDIENTS

Serves 4

350g/12oz/3 cups wholewheat
    pasta twists
225g/8oz/1½ cups green beans
8 rashers lean smoked back
    bacon, rind and fat removed
350g/12oz cherry tomatoes, halved
2 bunches spring onions, chopped
400g/14oz can chick-peas, rinsed
    and drained
90ml/6 tbsp tomato juice
30ml/2 tbsp balsamic vinegar
5ml/1 tsp ground cumin
5ml/1 tsp ground coriander
30ml/2 tbsp chopped
    fresh coriander
salt and ground black pepper

1 Cook the pasta in a large saucepan of lightly salted, boiling water for about 10–12 minutes until *al dente*. Meanwhile, trim and halve the green beans and cook them in boiling water for about 5 minutes until tender. Drain thoroughly and keep warm.

2 Preheat the grill and cook the bacon for 2–3 minutes on each side until cooked. Dice the bacon and add to the beans.

3 Put the tomatoes, spring onions and chick-peas in a bowl and mix together. In a small bowl, mix together the tomato juice, vinegar, spices, fresh coriander and seasoning, and pour over the tomato mixture.

--- COOK'S TIP ---

Always rinse any canned pulses that you use thoroughly before adding them to the dish in order to remove as much of the brine (salt water) as possible.

4 Drain the pasta thoroughly and add to the tomato mixture with the beans and bacon. Toss all the ingredients together to mix and serve warm or cold.

--- NUTRITION NOTES ---

Per portion:
Energy	444kcals/1892kJ
Protein	28.43g
Fat	8.67g
Saturated fat	1.98g
Carbohydrate	68.69g
Fibre	13.43g
Added sugar	0.00g
Sodium	1.26g

Bean and Ham Lasagne

Serve this scrumptious lasagne with a light and wholesome salad and fresh bread.

INGREDIENTS

Serves 6

10ml/2 tsp olive oil
350g/12oz/3 cups leeks, sliced
1 garlic clove, crushed
225g/8oz/3 cups
    mushrooms, sliced
2 courgettes, sliced
350g/12oz baby broad beans
350g/12oz/2 cups lean smoked
    ham, diced
75ml/5 tbsp chopped fresh parsley
30ml/2 tbsp chopped fresh chives
50g/2oz/4 tbsp half-fat spread
50g/2oz/½ cup plain
    wholemeal flour
600ml/1 pint/2½ cups
    skimmed milk
300ml/½ pint/1¼ cups vegetable
    stock, cooled
175g/6oz low-fat cheese
5ml/1 tsp smooth mustard
225g/8oz wholewheat lasagne
25g/1oz/½ cup fresh
    wholemeal breadcrumbs
15ml/1 tbsp grated Parmesan cheese
salt and ground black pepper
fresh herb sprigs, to garnish

2 Remove the pan from the heat, and stir in the broad beans, ham and herbs. Set aside.

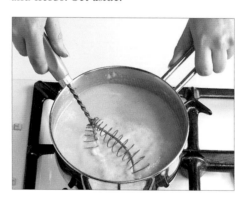

3 Make the cheese sauce. Put the half-fat spread, flour, milk and stock in a heavy-based saucepan and heat gently, whisking continuously, until the sauce comes to the boil and thickens. Simmer gently for 3 minutes, stirring. Grate the cheese.

5 Spoon half the ham mixture over the base of a shallow ovenproof dish or baking tin. Cover this with half the pasta. Repeat these layers with the remaining ham mixture and pasta, then pour the reserved cheese sauce over the pasta to cover it completely.

6 Mix together the fresh wholemeal breadcrumbs and the grated Parmesan cheese, and sprinkle this mixture over the lasagne. Bake for 45–60 minutes until the lasagne is cooked and golden brown on top. Garnish with fresh herb sprigs and serve immediately.

1 Preheat the oven to 180°C/350°F/ Gas 4. Heat the oil in a saucepan, add the leeks and garlic and cook for 3 minutes until softened, stirring constantly. Add the mushrooms and courgettes and cook for 5 minutes, stirring occasionally.

4 Remove the pan from the heat, add the mustard and grated cheese and stir until the cheese has melted and is well blended. Season to taste. Reserve 450 ml/¾ pint/scant 2 cups of cheese sauce and set aside. Mix the remaining sauce with the ham and vegetables.

— NUTRITION NOTES —	
Per portion:	
Energy	448kcals/1892kJ
Protein	38.45g
Fat	13.05g
Saturated fat	5.07g
Carbohydrate	46.16g
Fibre	10.86g
Added sugar	0.02g
Sodium	0.50g

Chicken and Bean Bake

A delicious combination of chicken, tarragon and mixed beans with a potato topping.

Ingredients

Serves 6

900g/2 lb potatoes
50g/2oz/½ cup reduced-fat mature
  Cheddar cheese, finely grated
600ml/1 pint/2½ cups plus
  30–45ml/2–3 tbsp skimmed milk
30ml/2 tbsp chopped fresh chives
2 leeks, washed and sliced
1 onion, sliced
30ml/2 tbsp dry white wine
40g/1½oz/3 tbsp half-fat spread
40g/1½oz/⅓ cup plain
  wholemeal flour
300ml/½ pint/1¼ cups chicken
  stock, cooled
350g/12oz cooked skinless, boneless
  chicken breast, diced
225g/8oz/3 cups brown-cap
  mushrooms, sliced
300g/11oz can red kidney beans
400g/14oz can flageolet beans
400g/14oz can black-eyed beans
30–45ml/2–3 tbsp chopped
  fresh tarragon
salt and ground black pepper

1 Preheat the oven to 200°C/400°F/ Gas 6. Cut the potatoes into chunks and cook in lightly salted, boiling water for 15–20 minutes, until tender. Drain and mash. Add the cheese, 30–45ml/2–3 tbsp milk and chives, season to taste and mix well. Keep warm and set aside.

2 Meanwhile, put the leeks and onion in a saucepan with the wine. Cover and cook gently for 10 minutes, until the vegetables are just tender, stirring occasionally.

3 In the meantime, put the half-fat spread, flour, remaining milk and stock in a saucepan. Heat gently, whisking continuously, until the sauce comes to the boil and thickens. Simmer gently for 3 minutes, stirring.

4 Remove the pan from the heat and add the leek mixture, chicken and mushrooms and mix well.

Variation

Sweet potatoes in place of standard potatoes work just as well in this recipe, and turkey or lean ham can be used instead of the chicken for a change.

5 Rinse and drain all the beans and add to the sauce. Stir in the tarragon and seasoning to taste. Heat gently, until the chicken mixture is piping hot, stirring.

6 Transfer the hot chicken and bean mixture to an ovenproof dish. Then spoon or pipe the mashed potato over the top so that it covers the filling completely. Put the dish in the oven and bake for about 30 minutes, until the potato topping is crisp and golden brown. Serve immediately.

Nutrition Notes

Per portion:

Energy	541kcals/2281kJ
Protein	44.98g
Fat	9.36g
Saturated fat	2.85g
Carbohydrate	72.49g
Fibre	16.46g
Added sugar	0.01g
Sodium	0.62g

Country Chicken Casserole

Succulent chicken joints are cooked in a rich vegetable sauce, and are particularly good served with brown rice.

INGREDIENTS

Serves 4
2 chicken breasts, skinned
2 chicken legs, skinned
30ml/2 tbsp plain wholemeal flour
15ml/1 tbsp sunflower oil
300ml/½ pint/1¼ cups chicken stock
300ml/½ pint/1¼ cups white wine
30ml/2 tbsp passata
15ml/1 tbsp tomato purée
4 rashers lean smoked back bacon
1 large onion, sliced
1 garlic clove, crushed
1 green pepper, seeded and sliced
225g/8oz/3 cups
   button mushrooms
225g/8oz carrots, sliced
1 bouquet garni
225g/8oz frozen Brussels sprouts
175g/6oz/1½ cups frozen petit pois
salt and ground black pepper
chopped fresh parsley, to garnish
brown rice, to serve

1 Preheat the oven to 180°C/350°F/ Gas 4. Coat the chicken joints with seasoned flour.

VARIATION

Use fresh Brussels sprouts and peas if they are available, and use red wine in place of white for a change.

2 Heat the oil in a large, flameproof casserole, add the chicken and cook until browned. Remove the chicken, using a slotted spoon, and set aside.

3 Add the remaining flour to the pan and cook for 1 minute. Gradually stir in the stock and wine, then add the passata and tomato purée.

4 Bring to the boil, stirring continuously, then add the chicken, bacon, onion, garlic, green pepper, mushrooms, carrots and bouquet garni and stir. Cover and bake in the oven for 1½ hours, stirring once or twice.

5 Stir in the Brussels sprouts and petit pois, re-cover and bake for a further 30 minutes.

6 Remove and discard the bouquet garni. Add seasoning to the casserole, garnish with the chopped fresh parsley and serve with brown rice.

NUTRITION NOTES

Per portion:
Energy	360kcals/1515kJ
Protein	37.83g
Fat	9.00g
Saturated fat	2.11g
Carbohydrate	21.55g
Fibre	8.51g
Added sugar	0.01g
Sodium	0.71g

Salmon and Broccoli Pilaff

This pilaff is an excellent choice for an informal suppertime meal.

INGREDIENTS

Serves 4

1 red onion, chopped
1 garlic clove, crushed
4 celery sticks, chopped
1 yellow pepper, seeded and diced
225g/8oz/1 cup brown basmati rice
600ml/1 pint/2½ cups fish stock
300ml/½ pint/1¼ cups white wine
400g/14oz can pink salmon,
   drained and flaked
400g/14oz can red kidney
   beans, rinsed and drained
350g/12oz small broccoli florets
45ml/3 tbsp chopped fresh parsley
15–30ml/1–2 tbsp light soy sauce
salt and ground black pepper
25g/1oz toasted flaked almonds,
   to garnish

1 Put the onion, garlic, celery, pepper, rice, stock and wine in a saucepan and bring to the boil, stirring. Simmer, uncovered, for 25–30 minutes, until almost all the liquid has been absorbed, stirring occasionally.

2 Stir the salmon and kidney beans into the rice mixture. Cook gently for a further 5–10 minutes, until the pilaff is piping hot.

3 Meanwhile, cook the broccoli florets in boiling water for about 5 minutes, until tender. Drain thoroughly and keep warm.

4 Fold the broccoli gently into the pilaff, then stir in the parsley and soy sauce, and season to taste. Garnish with toasted flaked almonds and serve immediately.

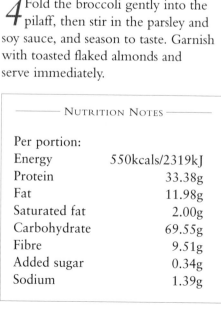

NUTRITION NOTES

Per portion:

Energy	550kcals/2319kJ
Protein	33.38g
Fat	11.98g
Saturated fat	2.00g
Carbohydrate	69.55g
Fibre	9.51g
Added sugar	0.34g
Sodium	1.39g

Oatmeal-crusted Mackerel

An appetizing way of serving fresh mackerel. Accompany with baked potatoes and cooked mangetouts for a tasty and filling meal.

INGREDIENTS

Serves 4

4 mackerel, each weighing about
   175–225g/6–8oz
juice of 1 lemon
50g/2oz/½ cup fine oatmeal
50g/2oz/½ cup medium oatmeal
30ml/2 tbsp chopped fresh
   mixed herbs
salt and ground black pepper
tomato quarters and fresh herb
   sprigs, to garnish
jacket potatoes and mangetouts, to serve

1 Remove and discard the heads from the mackerel, then clean the fish thoroughly.

2 Sprinkle the inside of each mackerel with lemon juice and season according to taste.

3 Mix together the two oatmeals and herbs, and press the oatmeal mixture firmly on to the outside of each fish.

VARIATION

Fresh sardines or trout can be used in place of the mackerel in this recipe and are equally tasty.

4 Preheat the grill. Grill the fish under a fairly high heat for 6–8 minutes, turning once, until it is tender and is just beginning to flake. Garnish with tomato quarters and fresh herb sprigs and serve with jacket potatoes and mangetouts.

NUTRITION NOTES

Per portion:

Energy	480kcals/2001kJ
Protein	36.30gg
Fat	30.15g
Saturated fat	6.18g
Carbohydrate	16.63g
Fibre	1.88g
Added sugar	0.00g
Sodium	0.10g

Tuna, Chick-pea and Cherry Tomato Salad

This healthy salad is easy to prepare and makes a light, satisfying meal when served with wholemeal bread. Only a little oil is used for the dressing, but it is very flavoursome.

INGREDIENTS

Serves 6

5ml/1 tsp olive oil
1 garlic clove, crushed
5ml/1 tsp ground coriander
5ml/1 tsp garam masala
5ml/1 tsp hot chilli powder
120ml/4fl oz/½ cup tomato juice
30ml/2 tbsp balsamic vinegar
dash of Tabasco sauce
675g/1½ lb cherry tomatoes, halved
½ cucumber, sliced
1 bunch radishes, sliced
1 bunch spring onions, chopped
50g/2oz watercress
2 x 400g/14oz cans chick-peas,
   rinsed and drained
400g/14oz can tuna in brine,
   drained and flaked
15ml/1 tbsp chopped fresh parsley
15ml/1 tbsp chopped fresh chives
salt and ground black pepper

1 Heat the oil in a small saucepan. Add the garlic and spices and cook gently for 1 minute, stirring.

2 Stir in the tomato juice, vinegar and Tabasco sauce, and heat gently until the mixture is boiling. Remove the pan from the heat and set aside to cool slightly.

3 Put the tomatoes and cucumber in a serving bowl.

4 Add the prepared radishes, spring onions and watercress to the tomato mixture.

5 Gently stir in the chick-peas, the tuna and the herbs.

6 Pour the tomato dressing over the salad and toss the ingredients together to mix. Season and serve.

— NUTRITION NOTES —	
Per portion:	
Energy	198kcals/839kJ
Protein	20.98g
Fat	4.30g
Saturated Fat	0.62g
Carbohydrate	20.70g
Fibre	5.88g
Added Sugar	0.00g
Sodium	0.45g

Spicy Seafood and Okra Stew

This spicy seafood dish is good accompanied by herbed brown rice. Heat the seafood mixture until piping hot before serving.

INGREDIENTS

Serves 4–6
10ml/2 tsp olive oil
1 onion, chopped
1 garlic clove, crushed
2 celery sticks, chopped
1 red pepper, seeded and diced
5ml/1 tsp each ground coriander,
    ground cumin and ground ginger
2.5ml/½ tsp hot chilli powder
2.5ml/½ tsp garam masala
30ml/2 tbsp plain wholemeal flour
300ml/½ pint/1¼ cups each
    fish stock and dry white wine
225g/8oz can chopped tomatoes
225g/8oz okra, trimmed and sliced
225g/8oz/3 cups
    mushrooms, sliced
450g/1 lb frozen cooked, shelled
    seafood, defrosted
175g/6oz/1 cup frozen
    sweetcorn kernels
225g/8oz/1 cup long grain
    brown rice
30–45ml/2–3 tbsp chopped fresh
    mixed herbs
salt and ground black pepper
flat leaf parsley sprigs, to garnish

1 Heat the oil in a large saucepan. Add the onion, garlic, celery and red pepper and cook for 5 minutes, stirring occasionally.

2 Add the spices and cook for 1 minute, stirring, then add the flour and cook for a further 1 minute, continuing to stir.

3 Gradually stir in the stock and wine and add the tomatoes, okra and mushrooms. Bring to the boil, stirring continuously, then cover and simmer for 20 minutes, stirring occasionally.

4 Stir in the seafood and sweetcorn. Cook for 10–15 minutes until hot.

5 Meanwhile, cook the brown rice in a large saucepan of lightly salted, boiling water for about 35 minutes, until just tender.

6 Rinse the cooked rice in fresh boiling water and drain thoroughly. Then toss the rice together with the mixed herbs to mix well. Finally, season the stew and serve on a bed of the herbed rice. Garnish with flat leaf parsley sprigs.

— NUTRITION NOTES —	
Per portion:	
Energy	541kcals/2284kJ
Protein	34.96g
Fat	7.18g
Saturated fat	1.42g
Carbohydrate	76.05g
Fibre	7.25g
Added sugar	0.01g
Sodium	1.35g

Salmon, Courgette and Sweetcorn Frittata

Serve this unusual frittata as a delicious and exciting change from an omelette, with a mixed tomato and pepper salad and warm wholemeal bread rolls.

INGREDIENTS

Serves 4–6
10ml/2 tsp olive oil
1 onion, chopped
175g/6oz/1⅓ cups courgettes,
    thinly sliced
225g/8oz boiled potatoes (with
    skins left on), diced
3 eggs, plus 2 egg whites
30ml/2 tbsp skimmed milk
200g/7oz can pink salmon in brine,
    drained and flaked
200g/7oz can sweetcorn
    kernels, drained
10ml/2 tsp dried mixed herbs
50g/2oz/½ cup reduced-fat mature
    Cheddar cheese, finely grated
salt and ground black pepper
chopped fresh mixed herbs and
    basil leaves, to garnish
pepper and tomato salad, to serve

2 Add the potatoes and cook for 5 minutes, stirring occasionally.

3 Beat the eggs, egg whites and milk together, add the salmon, sweetcorn, dried herbs and seasoning to taste and pour the mixture evenly over the vegetables.

4 Cook over a medium heat until the eggs are beginning to set and the frittata has begun to turn golden brown underneath.

5 Preheat the grill. Sprinkle the cheese over the frittata and place it under a medium heat until the cheese has melted and the top is golden brown.

6 Sprinkle the cooked frittata with plenty of chopped fresh herbs, and garnish with basil leaves. Serve the frittata immediately, while hot, cut into wedges and accompanied by a pepper and tomato salad.

1 Heat the oil in a large, non-stick frying pan. Add the onion and courgettes, and cook for 5 minutes, stirring occasionally.

VARIATION

Use canned tuna or crab in place of the salmon, if you like.

NUTRITION NOTES

Per portion:
Energy	336kcals/1415kJ
Protein	25.85g
Fat	12.20g
Saturated fat	3.57g
Carbohydrate	32.83g
Fibre	4.34g
Added sugar	0.00g
Sodium	0.49g

VEGETARIAN DISHES

Vegetarians have a head start on the rest of us when it comes to fibre in the diet, since they already value vegetables, pulses, pasta, rice, nuts and seeds, and consume plenty of wholefoods. Most vegetarians naturally eat a healthy, well-balanced diet. However, there are still some who take the soft option, plumping for processed foods like white rice or pasta swamped in cream sauce and topped with cheese. For them, this chapter offers fabulous fibre-rich alternatives, such as Vegetable Paella or Courgette, Sweetcorn and Plum Tomato Pizza. Recipes like Sweet-and-sour Mixed Bean Hot-pot and Vegetable Chilli prove that a vegetarian meal can be just as substantial and filling as one using meat. Whatever your preference, though, these delicious dishes are all guaranteed to go down well!

Vegetable Paella

This recipe makes a delicious change from the traditional, seafood-based paella.

INGREDIENTS

Serves 6

1 onion, chopped
2 garlic cloves, crushed
225g/8oz/2 cups leeks, sliced
3 celery sticks, chopped
1 red pepper, seeded and sliced
2 courgettes, sliced
175g/6oz/2¼ cups brown-cap
  mushrooms, sliced
400g/14oz can cannellini beans
175g/6oz/1½ cups frozen peas
450g/1 lb/2¼ cups long grain
  brown rice
900ml/1½ pints/3¾ cups
  vegetable stock
60ml/4 tbsp dry white wine
a few saffron strands
225g/8oz cherry tomatoes, halved
45–60ml/3–4 tbsp fresh mixed herbs
salt and ground black pepper
celery leaves and cherry tomatoes,
  to garnish
lemon wedges, to serve

1 Put the onion, garlic, leeks, celery, pepper, courgettes and mushrooms in a large saucepan and mix together.

2 Rinse and drain the canellini beans. Add them to the pan with the peas, rice, stock, wine and saffron.

3 Cover, bring to the boil, stirring. Simmer, uncovered, for about 35 minutes, until almost all the liquid has been absorbed and the rice is tender, stirring occasionally.

4 Finally, stir in the halved cherry tomatoes. Chop the herbs and add them to the pan. Season according to taste. Serve the paella immediately, garnished with celery leaves and cherry tomatoes and accompanied by lemon wedges for squeezing.

--- NUTRITION NOTES ---

Per portion:

Energy	416kcals/1759kJ
Protein	13.69g
Fat	3.95g
Saturated fat	0.86g
Carbohydrate	84.87g
Fibre	8.85g
Added sugar	0.03g
Sodium	0.54g

Vegetable Chilli

This vegetarian alternative to traditional chilli con carne is particularly good served with brown rice and natural yogurt.

INGREDIENTS

Serves 4

2 onions, chopped
1 garlic clove, crushed
3 celery sticks, chopped
1 green pepper, seeded and diced
225g/8oz/3 cups
    mushrooms, sliced
2 courgettes, diced
400g/14oz can red kidney beans, rinsed
    and drained
400g/14oz can chopped tomatoes
150ml/¼ pint/⅔ cup passata
30ml/2 tbsp tomato purée
15ml/1 tbsp tomato ketchup
5ml/1 tsp each hot chilli powder,
    ground cumin and ground coriander
salt and ground black pepper
fresh coriander sprigs, to garnish
brown rice, natural yogurt and cayenne
    pepper, to serve

1 Put the onions, garlic, celery, green pepper, mushrooms and courgettes in a large saucepan and mix together well.

2 Add the kidney beans, tomatoes, passata, tomato purée and tomato ketchup. Stir in the chilli powder, cumin, coriander and seasoning, and mix thoroughly.

3 Cover, bring to the boil and simmer for 20–30 minutes, stirring occasionally, until the vegetables are tender. Garnish with fresh coriander sprigs. Serve with brown rice and natural yogurt, sprinkled with cayenne pepper.

NUTRITION NOTES	
Per portion:	
Energy	158kcals/667kJ
Protein	9.96g
Fat	1.59g
Saturated fat	0.27g
Carbohydrate	27.55g
Fibre	8.58g
Added sugar	0.57g
Sodium	0.39g

Cheese, Onion and Mushroom Flan

A well-flavoured savoury flan, this is excellent served with slices of fresh wholemeal bread and a mixed-leaf salad for extra fibre, vitamins and minerals.

INGREDIENTS

Serves 6

175g/6oz/1½ cups plain wholemeal flour
a pinch of salt
75g/3oz/6 tbsp polyunsaturated margarine
1 onion, sliced
1 leek, sliced
175g/6oz/2¼ cups mushrooms, chopped
30ml/2 tbsp vegetable stock
2 eggs
150ml/¼ pint/⅔ cup skimmed milk
115g/4oz frozen sweetcorn kernels
30ml/2 tbsp snipped fresh chives
15ml/1 tbsp chopped fresh parsley
75g/3oz/¾ cup reduced-fat mature Cheddar cheese, finely grated
salt and ground black pepper
chives and salad leaves, to garnish

1 Preheat the oven to 200°C/400°F/ Gas 6. Sift the flour and salt into a bowl. Rub the fat into the flour until the mixture resembles breadcrumbs.

COOK'S TIP

Make this savoury flan in advance and freeze for up to three months. Defrost thoroughly and reheat to serve.

2 Mix in enough cold water to form a soft, but not sticky, dough. Wrap and chill for 30 minutes.

3 Put the onion and leek into a saucepan. Add the mushrooms and vegetable stock and bring to the boil. Cover and cook gently for 10 minutes, until the vegetables are tender. Drain.

4 Roll the pastry out on a lightly floured surface and use to line a 20 cm/8 in flan tin or dish. Place on a baking sheet.

5 Spoon the vegetables over the base. Beat the eggs and milk together, add the sweetcorn, herbs, cheese and seasoning, and mix well.

6 Pour the egg, milk and cheese mixture over the vegetables. Bake for 20 minutes, then reduce the temperature to 180°C/350°F/Gas 4 and cook for a further 30 minutes, until the flan is set and lightly browned on top. Garnish with chives and salad leaves. Serve either warm or cold, as you prefer.

NUTRITION NOTES

Per portion:

Energy	295kcals/1237kJ
Protein	12.75g
Fat	15.52g
Saturated fat	4.10g
Carbohydrate	27.97g
Fibre	4.22g
Added sugar	0.00g
Sodium	0.27g

Sweet-and-sour Mixed Bean Hot-pot

This appetizing combination of beans and vegetables has a tasty sweet-and-sour sauce, topped with a delicious layer of tender sliced potatoes.

Ingredients

Serves 8

450g/1 lb unpeeled potatoes
15ml/1 tbsp olive oil
40g/1½oz/3 tbsp half-fat spread
40g/1½oz/⅓ cup plain
   wholemeal flour
300ml/½ pint/1¼ cups passata
150ml/¼ pint/⅔ cup unsweetened
   apple juice
60ml/4 tbsp each soft light brown
   sugar, tomato ketchup, dry sherry,
   cider vinegar and light soy sauce
400g/14oz can butter beans
400g/14oz can red kidney beans
400g/14oz can flageolet beans
400g/14oz can chick-peas
175g/6oz green beans, chopped
   and blanched
225g/8oz shallots, sliced and
   blanched
225g/8oz/3 cups mushrooms, sliced
15ml/1 tbsp each chopped fresh thyme
   and marjoram
salt and ground black pepper
fresh herb sprigs, to garnish

1 Preheat the oven to 200°C/400°F/ Gas 6. Thinly slice the potatoes and par-boil them for about 4 minutes. Drain thoroughly, then toss them in the oil so they are lightly coated all over and set aside.

2 Place the half-fat spread, flour, passata, apple juice, sugar, tomato ketchup, sherry, vinegar and soy sauce in a saucepan. Heat gently, whisking continuously, until the sauce comes to the boil and thickens. Simmer gently for 3 minutes, stirring.

3 Rinse and drain the canned butter beans, kidney beans, flageolet beans and chick-peas, and add these to the sauce with all the remaining ingredients, except the herb garnish. Mix together well.

— Nutrition Notes —	
Per portion:	
Energy	410kcals/1733kJ
Protein	17.36g
Fat	7.43g
Saturated fat	1.42g
Carbohydrate	70.40g
Fibre	12.52g
Added sugar	15.86g
Sodium	1.54g

4 Spoon the bean mixture into a wide casserole.

5 Arrange the potato slices over the top, completely covering the bean mixture.

6 Cover the dish with foil and bake in the oven for approximately 1 hour, until the potatoes are cooked and tender. Remove the foil for the last 20 minutes of the cooking time to lightly brown the potatoes. Serve immediately, garnished with fresh herb sprigs.

Courgette, Sweetcorn and Plum Tomato Pizza

This wholewheat pizza is both healthy and delicious. It can be served hot or cold with a mixed bean salad, and also makes an ideal picnic snack.

INGREDIENTS

Serves 6
225g/8oz/2 cups plain
   wholemeal flour
a pinch of salt
10ml/2 tsp baking powder
50g/2oz/4 tbsp polyunsaturated
   margarine
150ml/¼ pint/⅔ cup skimmed milk
30ml/2 tbsp tomato purée
10ml/2 tsp dried *herbes
   de Provence*
10ml/2 tsp olive oil
1 onion, sliced
1 garlic clove, crushed
2 small courgettes, sliced
115g/4oz/1½ cups
   mushrooms, sliced
115g/4oz/⅔ cup sweetcorn kernels,
   thawed if frozen
2 plum tomatoes, sliced
50g/2oz/½ cup reduced-fat Red
   Leicester cheese, finely grated
50g/2oz/½ cup mozzarella cheese,
   finely grated
salt and ground black pepper
basil sprigs, to garnish

1 Preheat the oven to 220°C/425°F/ Gas 7. Line a baking sheet with non-stick baking paper. Put the flour, salt and baking powder in a bowl and rub the fat lightly into the flour until the mixture resembles breadcrumbs.

2 Add enough milk to form a soft, but not sticky, dough and knead lightly. Roll the dough out on a lightly floured surface, to a circle about 25 cm/10 in in diameter.

3 Place the dough on the prepared baking sheet and make the edges slightly thicker than the centre. Spread the tomato purée over the base and sprinkle the herbs on top.

4 Heat the oil in a frying pan, add the onion, garlic, courgettes and mushrooms and cook gently for 10 minutes, stirring occasionally.

5 Spread the prepared vegetable mixture over the pizza base and sprinkle the sweetcorn and seasoning over the top. Then arrange the tomato slices on top.

6 Mix together the Red Leicester and mozzarella cheeses and sprinkle them over the pizza. Bake for about 25–30 minutes, until cooked and golden brown on top. Serve the pizza hot or cold in slices, garnished with the basil sprigs.

--- NUTRITION NOTES ---

Per portion:
Energy	291kcals/1222kJ
Protein	12.56g
Fat	12.35g
Saturated fat	3.69g
Carbohydrate	34.54g
Fibre	4.93g
Added sugar	0.00g
Sodium	0.25g

Vegetable and Macaroni Bake

A welcome change from macaroni cheese, this recipe is excellent served with steamed fresh vegetables.

INGREDIENTS

Serves 6

225g/8oz/2¼ cups
   wholewheat macaroni
225g/8oz/2 cups leeks, sliced
45ml/3 tbsp vegetable stock
225g/8oz broccoli florets
50g/2oz/4 tbsp half-fat spread
50g/2oz/½ cup plain
   wholemeal flour
900ml/1½ pints/3⅔ cups
   skimmed milk
150g/5oz/1¼ cups reduced-fat
   mature Cheddar cheese, grated
5ml/1 tsp prepared English mustard
350g/12 oz can sweetcorn kernels
25g/1oz/½ cup fresh
   wholemeal breadcrumbs
30ml/2 tbsp chopped fresh parsley
2 tomatoes, cut into eighths
salt and ground black pepper

1 Preheat the oven to 200°C/400°F/ Gas 6. Cook the macaroni in lightly salted, boiling water for about 10 minutes, until just tender, then drain and keep warm.

--- VARIATION ---

Use another reduced-fat hard cheese such as Red Leicester or Double Gloucester in place of the Cheddar cheese.

2 Cook the leeks in the stock for about 10 minutes, until tender, then strain and set aside. Blanch the broccoli in boiling water for 2 minutes, drain and set aside.

3 Put the half-fat spread, flour and milk in a saucepan. Heat gently, whisking continuously, until the sauce comes to the boil and thickens. Simmer gently for 3 minutes, stirring.

4 Remove the pan from the heat, add 115g/4oz/1 cup of the cheese and stir until it has melted and is well blended with the milk mixture.

5 Add the macaroni, leeks, broccoli, mustard, drained sweetcorn and seasoning and mix well. Transfer the mixture to an ovenproof dish.

6 Mix the remaining cheese, breadcrumbs and parsley together and sprinkle this mixture over the top. Arrange the tomatoes on top and then bake for about 30–40 minutes, until bubbling and golden brown on top. Serve the bake immediately, while piping hot.

--- NUTRITION NOTES ---

Per portion:

Energy	376kcals/1593kJ
Protein	23.30g
Fat	9.68g
Saturated fat	3.82g
Carbohydrate	52.34g
Fibre	7.12g
Added sugar	0.01g
Sodium	0.53g

Curried New Potato and Green Bean Salad

Tender new potatoes and green beans are tossed together in a light, subtly flavoured dressing to make this salad. If you want to make a plainer dish, leave out the curry paste.

INGREDIENTS

Serves 6

225g/8oz/1½ cups green beans, trimmed and halved
675g/1½ lb baby new potatoes, cooked in their skins
2 bunches spring onions, chopped
115g/4oz/¾ cup sultanas
75g/3oz/¾ cup ready-to-eat dried pears, finely chopped
90ml/6 tbsp reduced-calorie mayonnaise
60ml/4 tbsp low-fat plain yogurt
30ml/2 tbsp Greek yogurt
15ml/1 tbsp tomato purée
15ml/1 tbsp curry paste
30ml/2 tbsp snipped fresh chives
salt and ground black pepper

1 Cook the beans in boiling water for 5 minutes, until tender. Drain, then rinse under cold, running water to cool them quickly. Drain again.

2 Put the beans, potatoes, spring onions, sultanas and pears in a bowl and mix together.

3 In a small bowl, mix together the mayonnaise, yogurts, tomato purée, curry paste, chives and seasoning.

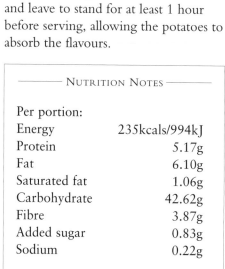

4 Add the dressing to the vegetables and toss together to mix. Cover and leave to stand for at least 1 hour before serving, allowing the potatoes to absorb the flavours.

NUTRITION NOTES	
Per portion:	
Energy	235kcals/994kJ
Protein	5.17g
Fat	6.10g
Saturated fat	1.06g
Carbohydrate	42.62g
Fibre	3.87g
Added sugar	0.83g
Sodium	0.22g

Spicy Bean and Lentil Loaf

This is an unusual meat-free and high fibre savoury loaf, perfect for a picnic.

INGREDIENTS

Serves 12

10ml/2 tsp olive oil
1 onion, finely chopped
1 garlic clove, crushed
2 celery sticks, finely chopped
400g/14oz can red kidney beans
400g/14oz can lentils
1 egg
1 carrot, coarsely grated
50g/2oz/½ cup hazelnuts,
   finely chopped
50g/2oz/½ cup reduced-fat mature
   Cheddar cheese, finely grated
50g/2oz/1 cup fresh
   wholemeal breadcrumbs
15ml/1 tbsp tomato purée
15ml/1 tbsp tomato ketchup
5ml/1 tsp each ground cumin, ground
   coriander and hot chilli powder
salt and ground black pepper
salad, to serve

1 Preheat the oven to 180°C/350°F/ Gas 4. Lightly grease a 900g/2 lb loaf tin. Heat the oil in a saucepan, add the onion, garlic and celery and cook for 5 minutes, stirring occasionally. Remove from the heat and cool a little.

2 Rinse and drain the beans and lentils. Process in a blender or food processor with the onion mixture and egg until smooth.

3 Transfer the bean and lentil mixture to a large bowl, add all the remaining ingredients and mix well. Season to taste.

— NUTRITION NOTES —	
Per portion:	
Energy	119kcals/499kJ
Protein	7.22g
Fat	4.85g
Saturated fat	0.88g
Carbohydrate	12.57g
Fibre	3.31g
Added sugar	0.19g
Sodium	0.17g

4 Spoon the mixture into the prepared tin and level the surface. Bake for about 1 hour, then remove from the tin and serve hot or cold in slices, accompanied by a salad.

Fruity Rice Salad

An appetizing and colourful rice salad that combines many different flavours.

INGREDIENTS

Serves 4-6

225g/8oz/1 cup mixed brown and
    wild rice
1 yellow pepper, seeded and diced
1 bunch spring onions, chopped
3 celery sticks, chopped
1 large beefsteak tomato, chopped
2 green-skinned eating
    apples, chopped
175g/6oz/¾ cup ready-to-eat dried
    apricots, chopped
115g/4oz/¾ cup raisins
30ml/2 tbsp unsweetened
    apple juice
30ml/2 tbsp dry sherry
30ml/2 tbsp light soy sauce
dash of Tabasco sauce
30ml/2 tbsp chopped fresh parsley
15ml/1 tbsp chopped fresh rosemary
salt and ground black pepper

1 Cook the rice in a large saucepan of lightly salted, boiling water for about 30 minutes (or according to the instructions on the packet), until tender. Rinse the rice under cold, running water to cool quickly and then drain thoroughly.

2 Place the yellow pepper, spring onions, celery, tomato, apples, apricots, raisins and the cooked rice in a serving bowl and mix well.

3 In a small bowl, mix together the apple juice, sherry, soy sauce, Tabasco sauce, herbs and seasoning.

4 Pour the dressing over the rice mixture and toss the ingredients together to mix. Serve immediately or cover and chill in the fridge before serving.

NUTRITION NOTES	
Per portion:	
Energy	428kcals/1817kJ
Protein	8.15g
Fat	2.50g
Saturated fat	0.52g
Carbohydrate	97.15g
Fibre	7.17g
Added sugar	0.31g
Sodium	0.58g

Bulgur Wheat and Broad Bean Salad

This summery salad is perfect served with fresh, crusty wholemeal bread and home-made chutney or pickle. For non-vegetarians it can be served as an accompaniment to grilled lean meat or fish.

INGREDIENTS

Serves 6

350g/12oz/2 cups bulgur wheat
225g/8oz frozen broad beans
115g/4oz/1 cup frozen petit pois
225g/8oz cherry tomatoes, halved
1 sweet onion, chopped
1 red pepper, seeded and diced
50g/2oz mangetouts, chopped
50g/2oz watercress
15ml/1 tbsp chopped fresh parsley
15ml/1 tbsp chopped fresh basil
15ml/1 tbsp chopped fresh thyme
fat-free French dressing
salt and ground black pepper

1 Soak and cook the bulgur wheat according to the packet instructions. Drain thoroughly and put into a serving bowl.

2 Meanwhile, cook the frozen broad beans and petits pois in lightly salted, boiling water for approximately 3 minutes, until tender. Drain them thoroughly and add to the prepared bulgur wheat.

NUTRITION NOTES	
Per portion:	
Energy	277kcals/1162kJ
Protein	11.13g
Fat	1.81g
Saturated fat	0.17g
Carbohydrate	55.34g
Fibre	4.88g
Added sugar	0.00g
Sodium	0.02g

3 Add the cherry tomatoes, onion, pepper, mangetouts and watercress to the bulgur wheat mixture and mix.

4 Add the herbs, seasoning and French dressing to taste, tossing the ingredients together. Serve immediately or cover and chill in the fridge before serving.

VARIATION
Use cooked couscous, boiled brown rice or wholewheat pasta in place of the bulgur wheat, if you prefer.

Roast Pepper and Wild Mushroom Pasta Salad

This pasta salad is colourful as well as highly nutritious.

INGREDIENTS

Serves 6

1 red pepper, halved
1 yellow pepper, halved
1 green pepper, halved
350g/12oz/3 cups wholewheat
    pasta shells or twists
30ml/2 tbsp olive oil
45ml/3 tbsp balsamic vinegar
75ml/5 tbsp tomato juice
30ml/2 tbsp chopped fresh basil
15ml/1 tbsp chopped fresh thyme
175g/6oz/2⅓ cups shiitake
    mushrooms, sliced
175g/6oz/2⅓ cups oyster
    mushrooms, sliced
400g/14oz can black-eyed beans,
    rinsed and drained
115g/4oz/¾ cup sultanas
2 bunches spring onions,
    finely chopped
salt and ground black pepper

1 Preheat the grill. Put all the halved peppers cut-side down on a grill pan rack and place under a hot grill for 10–15 minutes, until the skins are charred. Cover the peppers with a clean, damp tea towel and set aside to cool.

2 Meanwhile, cook the wholewheat pasta shells or twists in lightly salted, boiling water for approximately 10–12 minutes (or according to the instructions on the packet), until *al dente*, then drain thoroughly.

3 Mix together the oil, vinegar, tomato juice, basil and thyme, add to the warm pasta and toss together.

4 Remove and discard the skins from the red, yellow and green peppers: they should come away easily. Seed and slice the peppers and add to the pasta along with the mushrooms, beans, sultanas, spring onions and seasoning. Toss all the ingredients together in the bowl to mix well, and serve immediately. Alternatively, cover the salad bowl and chill in the fridge for several hours before serving.

— NUTRITION NOTES —	
Per portion:	
Energy	334kcals/1425kJ
Protein	13.58g
Fat	6.02g
Saturated fat	0.89g
Carbohydrate	60.74g
Fibre	9.37g
Added sugar	0.00g
Sodium	0.11g

Carrot, Raisin and Apricot Coleslaw

This is a high fibre coleslaw, combining cabbage, carrots and dried fruit in a nutritious light yogurt dressing.

INGREDIENTS

Serves 6

350g/12oz/3 cups white cabbage, finely shredded
225g/8oz/1½ cups carrots, coarsely grated
1 red onion, sliced
3 celery sticks, sliced
150g/5oz/1 cup raisins
75g/3oz/⅓ cup ready-to-eat dried apricots, chopped
120ml/4fl oz/½ cup reduced-calorie mayonnaise
90ml/6 tbsp low-fat plain yogurt
30ml/2 tbsp chopped fresh mixed herbs
salt and ground black pepper

1 Put the cabbage and carrots in a large bowl.

2 Add the onion, celery, raisins and apricots and mix well.

NUTRITION NOTES	
Per portion:	
Energy	204kcals/858kJ
Protein	3.71g
Fat	6.37g
Saturated fat	0.93g
Carbohydrate	35.04g
Fibre	4.25g
Added sugar	0.50g
Sodium	0.24g

3 In a small bowl, mix together the mayonnaise, yogurt, fresh herbs and seasoning.

VARIATION

Use other dried fruit such as sultanas and ready-to-eat dried pears or peaches instead of the raisins and apricots.

4 Add the mayonnaise dressing to the bowl and toss the ingredients together to mix. Cover and chill for several hours before serving.

HOT AND COLD DESSERTS

Delectable desserts are always tempting, but this does not mean that they need to be too unhealthy. There are plenty of ways to increase the fibre content of puddings and desserts. Fruit, whether fresh, dried or cooked, combines deliciously with wholewheat flours and wholemeal breads to make sweet treats such as Pineapple and Peach Upside-down Pudding or Peach and Raspberry Crumble. Such winter warmers are satisfying but may be somewhat substantial for sizzling summer days. If you prefer something light and luscious, try Tropical Fruit Filo Clusters or a scoop of Wholemeal Bread and Banana Yogurt Ice, which is a lot lighter than its name suggests. A mixture of dried and fresh fruit makes a superb sweet salad, as demonstrated by Apricot and Banana Compote, which is equally suitable for breakfast or after dinner.

Pineapple and Peach Upside-down Pudding

An inspired combination of pineapple and peaches, this old favourite goes well with ice cream, or even low-fat custard for a healthier alternative. It is also great fun to make.

INGREDIENTS

Serves 6

75ml/5 tbsp golden syrup
225g/8oz can pineapple chunks in
   fruit juice
175g/6oz/¾ cup ready-to-eat
   dried peaches, chopped
115g/4oz/⅔ cup caster sugar
115g/4oz/½ cup half-fat spread
175g/6oz/1½ cups self-raising
   wholemeal flour
5ml/1 tsp baking powder
2 eggs

1 Preheat the oven to 180°C/350°F/ Gas 4. Lightly grease an 18cm/ 7in, loose-bottomed, round cake tin and line the base with non-stick baking paper.

2 Heat the golden syrup gently in a saucepan and pour over the bottom of the tin.

3 Strain the pineapple, reserving 45ml/3 tbsp of the juice.

4 Mix together the pineapple and peaches and scatter them over the syrup layer in the tin.

5 Put the caster sugar, half-fat spread, flour, baking powder, eggs and reserved pineapple juice in a bowl and beat together until smooth.

6 Spread the pudding mixture evenly over the fruit and level the surface. Bake for about 45 minutes, until risen and golden brown. Turn out carefully on to a serving plate and serve hot or cold in slices.

VARIATION

Other combinations of canned and dried fruits, such as apricots and pears, peaches and figs or raspberries and dates, work just as well.

NUTRITION NOTES

Per portion:

Energy	410kcals/1733kJ
Protein	8.36g
Fat	10.69g
Saturated fat	2.82g
Carbohydrate	74.73g
Fibre	4.94g
Added sugar	37.51g
Sodium	0.21g

Peach and Raspberry Crumble

A scrumptious, quick and easy dessert, this crumble is good served hot or cold, on its own or with cream or yogurt.

INGREDIENTS

Serves 4

75g/3oz/⅔ cup plain
  wholemeal flour
75g/3oz/¾ cup medium oatmeal
75g/3oz/6 tbsp half-fat spread
50g/2oz/¼ cup soft light
  brown sugar
2.5ml/½ tsp ground cinnamon
400g/14oz can peach slices in
  fruit juice
225g/8oz/1⅓ cups raspberries
30ml/2 tbsp clear honey
raspberry leaves, to decorate

1 Preheat the oven to 180°C/350°F/ Gas 4. Put the flour and oatmeal in a bowl and mix together.

— VARIATION —

Use other combinations of fruit, depending on what is available.

2 Rub in the half-fat spread until the mixture resembles breadcrumbs, then stir in the sugar and cinnamon.

3 Drain the peach slices and reserve the juice.

4 Roughly chop the peaches and put them in an ovenproof dish, then scatter over the raspberries.

5 Mix together the reserved peach juice and honey, pour over the fruit and stir.

6 Spoon the crumble mixture over the fruit, pressing it down lightly. Bake for about 45 minutes, until golden brown on top. Serve hot or cold, as you prefer, decorated with raspberry leaves.

— NUTRITION NOTES —

Per portion:

Energy	334kcals/1413kJ
Protein	7.02g
Fat	9.9g
Saturated fat	2.51g
Carbohydrate	58.57g
Fibre	5.22g
Added sugar	12.66g
Sodium	0.14g

Fruit and Spice Bread Pudding

An easy-to-make fruity dessert with a hint of spice, this is a healthier, more fibre-rich version of the traditional pudding.

INGREDIENTS

Serves 4

6 medium slices wholemeal bread
50g/2oz reduced-sugar jam
50g/2oz/⅓ cup sultanas
50g/2oz/¼ cup ready-to-eat
   dried apricots, chopped
50g/2oz/¼ cup soft light
   brown sugar
5ml/1 tsp ground mixed spice
2 eggs
600ml/1 pint/2½ cups
   skimmed milk
finely grated rind of 1 lemon

1 Preheat the oven to 160°C/325°F/ Gas 3. Remove and discard the crusts from the slices of wholemeal bread. Spread the bread slices with a jam of your choice and cut them into small triangles. Place half the bread triangles in two long columns in a lightly greased ovenproof dish.

2 Mix together the sultanas, apricots, sugar and spice and sprinkle half the fruit mixture evenly over the bread in the dish.

3 Top with the remaining bread triangles and then sprinkle over the remaining fruit mixture.

4 Beat the eggs, milk and lemon rind together in a jug and pour over the bread. Set aside for 30 minutes to allow the bread to absorb some of the liquid. Bake for 45–60 minutes, until set and golden brown. Serve hot or cold.

--- NUTRITION NOTES ---

Per portion:

Energy	305kcals/1293kJ
Protein	13.77g
Fat	4.51g
Saturated fat	1.27g
Carbohydrate	56.38g
Fibre	3.75g
Added sugar	13.47g
Sodium	0.38g

Apricot and Banana Compote

This compote is delicious served on its own or with custard or ice cream. Served for breakfast with yogurt, it makes a tasty and nutritious start to the day.

INGREDIENTS

Serves 4

225g/8oz/1 cup ready-to-eat
    dried apricots
300ml/½ pint/1¼ cups unsweetened
    orange juice
150ml/¼ pint/⅔ cup unsweetened
    apple juice
5ml/1 tsp ground ginger
3 medium bananas
25g/1oz/¼ cup toasted
    flaked almonds

1 Put the apricots in a saucepan with the fruit juices and ginger and stir. Cover, bring to the boil and simmer gently for 10 minutes, stirring from time to time.

2 Set aside to cool, leaving the lid on. Slice the bananas into thick slices and stir them into the cooled, cooked apricot mixture.

3 Spoon the fruit and juices into a serving dish.

4 Serve this compote immediately, or cover and chill for several hours in the fridge before serving. Sprinkle with toasted flaked almonds, to serve.

VARIATION

Use other combinations of dried and fresh fruit such as prunes, figs, apples or peaches.

NUTRITION NOTES

Per portion:

Energy	241kcals/1022kJ
Protein	4.92g
Fat	4.18g
Saturated fat	0.37g
Carbohydrate	48.98g
Fibre	4.91g
Added sugar	0.00g
Sodium	0.02g

Tropical Fruit Filo Clusters

These fruity filo clusters make a great family treat or dinner-party dessert. They are delicious served hot or cold, either on their own or with cream.

INGREDIENTS

Makes 8

1 banana, sliced
1 small mango, peeled, stoned
   and diced
lemon juice, to sprinkle
1 small cooking apple,
   coarsely grated
6 fresh or dried dates, stoned
   and chopped
50g/2oz ready-to-eat dried
   pineapple, chopped
50g/2oz/⅓ cup sultanas
50g/2oz/¼ cup soft light
   brown sugar
5ml/1 tsp ground mixed spice
8 sheets filo pastry
30ml/2 tbsp sunflower oil
icing sugar, to serve

NUTRITION NOTES

Per portion:

Energy	197kcals/833kJ
Protein	3.09g
Fat	3.58g
Saturated fat	0.44g
Carbohydrate	40.21g
Fibre	2.31g
Added sugar	9.96g
Sodium	0.16g

1 Preheat the oven to 200°C/400°F/ Gas 6. Line a baking sheet with non-stick baking paper. Toss the banana and mango in lemon juice to prevent discoloration.

2 Add the apple, dates, pineapple, sultanas, sugar and spice, and mix.

3 For each cluster, cut each sheet of filo pastry in half. Cover when not in use to keep moist. Lightly brush two squares of pastry with oil and place one on top of the other at a 90° angle.

4 Spoon some fruit filling into the centre, gather the pastry up over the filling and secure with string. Place the cluster on the prepared baking sheet and lightly brush all over with oil.

5 Repeat with the remaining ingredients to make a total of eight fruit clusters. Bake for 25–30 minutes, until golden brown and crisp.

6 Carefully snip and discard the string from each cluster. Serve the clusters hot or cold, dusted with a little sifted icing sugar.

Winter Fruit Salad

A colourful, refreshing and nutritious fruit salad, which is wonderful served with Greek-style yogurt or cream.

INGREDIENTS

Serves 6

225g/8oz can pineapple chunks in
    fruit juice
200ml/7fl oz/scant 1 cup freshly
    squeezed orange juice
200ml/7fl oz/scant 1 cup unsweetened
    apple juice
30ml/2 tbsp orange or apple liqueur
30ml/2 tbsp clear honey (optional)
2 oranges, peeled
2 green-skinned eating
    apples, peeled and sliced
2 pears, peeled and sliced
4 plums, stoned and sliced
12 fresh dates, stoned and chopped
115g/4oz/½ cup ready-to-eat
    dried apricots, sliced
1 fresh mint sprig, to decorate

1 Drain the pineapple, reserving the juice. Put the juice from the pineapple, the orange juice, apple juice, liqueur and honey, if using, in a large serving bowl and stir to mix.

2 Segment the oranges, catching any juice in the bowl, and put the orange segments and pineapple in the fruit juice mixture.

3 Add the apples and pears to the bowl and mix well.

VARIATION

Use other unsweetened fruit juices such as pink grapefruit and pineapple juice in place of the orange and apple juice.

4 Stir in the plums, dates and apricots, cover and chill for several hours. Decorate with a fresh mint sprig before serving.

--- NUTRITION NOTES ---

Per portion:

Energy	227kcals/967kJ
Protein	2.85g
Fat	0.37g
Saturated fat	0.00g
Carbohydrate	53.68g
Fibre	5.34g
Added sugar	1.33g
Sodium	0.01g

Wholemeal Bread and Banana Yogurt Ice

Serve this tempting yogurt ice with seasonal fresh fruit and some wafer biscuits for a tasty, light dessert.

INGREDIENTS

Serves 6

115g/4oz/2 cups fresh wholemeal breadcrumbs
50g/2oz/¼ cup soft light brown sugar
300ml/½ pint/1¼ cups cold low-fat ready-made custard
150g/5oz/generous 1 cup low-fat fromage frais
150g/5oz/generous 1 cup Greek-style yogurt
4 bananas
juice of 1 lemon
25g/1oz/¼ cup icing sugar, sifted
50g/2oz/⅓ cup raisins, chopped
pared lemon rind, to decorate
strawberries and biscuits, to serve

1 Preheat the oven to 200°C/400°F/ Gas 6. Mix together the breadcrumbs and brown sugar and spread the mixture out on a non-stick baking sheet. Bake for about 10 minutes, until crisp, stirring occasionally. Set aside to cool, then break the mixture up into crumbs.

2 Meanwhile, put the custard, fromage frais and yogurt in a bowl and mix thoroughly. Mash the bananas with the lemon juice and add to the custard mixture, stirring well. Fold in the icing sugar.

3 Pour the mixture into a shallow, freezerproof container and leave to freeze for about 3 hours, or until the mixture has become mushy in consistency. Spoon into a chilled bowl and quickly mash the chunks up with a fork in order to break down the ice crystals.

4 Add the breadcrumbs and raisins and mix well. Return the mixture to the container, cover and freeze until firm. Transfer to the fridge 30 minutes before serving, to soften a little. Decorate with lemon rind and serve with strawberries and biscuits.

NUTRITION NOTES	
Per portion:	
Energy	277kcals/1170kJ
Protein	7.55g
Fat	5.51g
Saturated fat	2.99g
Carbohydrate	52.27g
Fibre	2.01g
Added sugar	12.77g
Sodium	0.17g

CAKES AND BAKES

Bran is the obvious ingredient for boosting the fibre content of cakes and bakes, but it is by no means the only candidate. Although Pear and Sultana Bran Muffins and Banana Bran Loaf are both temptingly tasty, Carrot and Coconut Cake has more fibre per portion than either, and is beautifully moist and flavoursome. Another moist and fruity bake is Farmhouse Apple and Sultana Cake, while Date and Orange Slices are gloriously chewy and popular with children. Rock cakes may seem old-fashioned, but making them with wholemeal flour and grated lemon rind brings them bang up-to-date. On the savoury front, try Cheese and Herb Wholewheat Soda Bread or, for an afternoon snack, enjoy Cheese and Pineapple Wholewheat Scones. Both are delicious toasted and served with low-fat spread.

Pear and Sultana Bran Muffins

These mouthwatering muffins are a real delight. They are best eaten freshly baked and perhaps spread with a little butter or low-fat spread and honey.

INGREDIENTS

Makes 12

75g/3oz/⅔ cup plain wholemeal flour, sifted
50g/2oz/½ cup plain white flour, sifted
50g/2oz/2½ cups bran
15ml/1 tbsp baking powder, sifted
pinch of salt
50g/2oz/4 tbsp half-fat spread
50g/2oz/¼ cup soft light brown sugar
1 egg
200ml/7fl oz/scant 1 cup skimmed milk
50g/2oz/½ cup ready-to-eat dried pears, chopped
50g/2oz/⅓ cup sultanas

1 Preheat the oven to 200°C/400°F/ Gas 6. Lightly grease 12 muffin or deep-cup bun tins or line them with paper muffin cases. Mix together the wholemeal and white flours, bran, baking powder and salt in a bowl.

2 Gently heat the half-fat spread in a saucepan until melted.

3 Mix together the melted fat, sugar, egg and milk in a jug and pour over the dry ingredients.

4 Using a spoon or spatula, gently fold the ingredients together, but only enough to combine them. The mixture should look quite lumpy as over-mixing will result in particularly heavy muffins.

5 Fold the pears and sultanas into the mixture.

6 Spoon the mixture in equal sized portions into the prepared muffin or bun tins. Bake for approximately 15–20 minutes, until they are well risen and have turned golden brown. Turn the cakes out on to a wire rack and leave to cool before serving.

COOK'S TIP

For a quick and easy way to chop dried fruit, snip with kitchen scissors.

NUTRITION NOTES

Per portion:	
Energy	108kcals/455kJ
Protein	3.40g
Fat	2.68g
Saturated fat	0.70g
Carbohydrate	18.84g
Fibre	2.64g
Added sugar	4.37g
Sodium	0.15g

Banana Bran Loaf

A tempting and filling teatime treat, this loaf is delicious served in slices, either on its own or with a little butter.

INGREDIENTS

Serves 12

115g/4oz/½ cup half-fat spread
115g/4oz/½ cup soft light
    brown sugar
3 eggs, beaten
175g/6oz/1½ cups self-raising
    wholemeal flour, sifted
50g/2oz/2½ cups bran
5ml/1 tsp baking powder, sifted
pinch of salt
5–10ml/1–2 tsp ground ginger
3 medium bananas, mashed
175g/6oz/1 cup raisins

1 Preheat the oven to 180°C/350°F/ Gas 4. Lightly grease a 900g/2 lb loaf tin and line the base with non-stick baking paper.

2 Put the half-fat spread, sugar, eggs, flour, bran, baking powder, salt and ground ginger in a bowl and beat together, using a wooden spoon or electric mixer, until it has been thoroughly mixed.

3 Add the mashed bananas to the cake mixture and beat until well mixed. Fold in the raisins.

4 Spoon the mixture into the prepared tin and level the surface.

5 Bake the loaf for about 1¼ hours, until it is well risen, golden brown and firm to the touch. Cool in the tin for a few minutes, then turn out on to a wire rack to cool completely. Serve in slices, either warm or cold, whichever you prefer.

— NUTRITION NOTES —	
Per portion:	
Energy	211kcals/891kJ
Protein	5.42g
Fat	6.11g
Saturated fat	1.63g
Carbohydrate	36.30g
Fibre	3.40g
Added sugar	9.71g
Sodium	0.09g

Fruity Muesli Bars

These fruity muesli bars make an appetizing snack at any time of day. When they are cool, keep them moist by sealing them with cling film.

INGREDIENTS

Makes 10–12

115g/4oz/8 tbsp half-fat spread
75g/3oz/⅓ cup soft light
  brown sugar
45ml/3 tbsp golden syrup
150g/5oz/1¼ cups Swiss-style muesli,
  with no added sugar
50g/2oz/½ cup rolled oats
5ml/1 tsp ground mixed spice
50g/2oz/⅓ cup sultanas
50g/2oz/½ cup ready-to-eat dried
  pears, chopped

1 Preheat the oven to 180°C/350°F/ Gas 4. Lightly grease an 18cm/7in square cake tin.

2 Put the half-fat spread, sugar and syrup in a saucepan and gently heat until melted and blended, stirring.

3 Remove the pan from the heat, add the muesli, oats, spice, sultanas and pears, and mix well.

4 Transfer the mixture to the prepared tin and level the surface, pressing down.

5 Bake for 20–30 minutes, until golden brown. Cool slightly in the tin, then mark into bars using a sharp knife. When firm, remove the muesli bars from the tin and cool on a wire rack.

NUTRITION NOTES

Per portion:

Energy	191kcals/804kJ
Protein	3.09g
Fat	6.26g
Saturated fat	1.59g
Carbohydrate	32.57g
Fibre	1.66g
Added sugar	10.14g
Sodium	0.11g

VARIATION

A combination of rolled oats and oatmeal can be used in place of muesli for a delicious change. The dried fruit helps to make the bars more naturally sweet.

Carrot and Coconut Cake

A satisfying cake with a delicious combination of flavours.

INGREDIENTS

Serves 10
115g/4oz/½ cup half-fat spread
115g/4oz/generous ½ cup caster sugar
2 eggs
175g/6oz/1½ cups self-raising
   wholemeal flour, sifted
50g/2oz/2½ cups bran
5ml/1 tsp baking powder, sifted
90ml/6 tbsp skimmed milk, plus a little
   extra to mix
225g/8oz/1⅔ cups carrots,
   coarsely grated
115g/4oz/1 cup desiccated coconut
50g/2oz/⅓ cup sultanas
finely grated rind of 1 orange
15–30ml/1–2 tbsp golden
   granulated sugar

1 Preheat the oven to 180°C/350°F/ Gas 4. Lightly grease a deep, 18cm/7in round cake tin and line with some non-stick baking paper. Put the half-fat spread, caster sugar, eggs, flour, bran, baking powder and milk in a large mixing bowl. Using an electric mixer, if you like, beat all the ingredients together until they are thoroughly mixed.

2 Fold in the carrots, coconut, sultanas and orange rind, plus extra milk if needed, to make a soft dropping consistency.

3 Spoon the mixture into the prepared tin and level the surface.

4 Sprinkle the top with granulated sugar and bake for about 1 hour, until risen, golden brown and firm to the touch. Cool in the tin for a few minutes, then turn out on to a wire rack to cool completely before cutting it into slices.

——— NUTRITION NOTES ———	
Per portion:	
Energy	280kcals/1175kJ
Protein	6.25g
Fat	13.78g
Saturated fat	7.91g
Carbohydrate	35.17g
Fibre	5.61g
Added sugar	16.13g
Sodium	0.11g

Farmhouse Apple and Sultana Cake

A slice of this moist and lightly spiced fruit cake makes the perfect treat with a cup of tea. You could also have some for breakfast with natural yogurt.

INGREDIENTS

Serves 12

175g/6oz/¾ cup half-fat spread
175g/6oz/¾ cup soft light
   brown sugar
3 eggs
225g/8oz/2 cups self-raising
   wholemeal flour, sifted
115g/4oz/1 cup self-raising white
   flour, sifted
5ml/1 tsp baking powder, sifted
10ml/2 tsp ground mixed spice
350g/12oz cooking apples, peeled,
   cored and diced
175g/6oz/1 cup sultanas
75ml/5 tbsp skimmed milk
30ml/2 tbsp demerara sugar

1 Preheat the oven to 160°C/325°F/ Gas 3. Lightly grease a deep, 20cm/8in round, loose-bottomed cake tin and line with non-stick baking paper. Put the half-fat spread, soft brown sugar, eggs, flours, baking powder and spice in a bowl and beat well together until thoroughly mixed.

2 Fold in the apples, sultanas and sufficient milk to make a soft dropping consistency.

3 Spoon the mixture into the prepared tin and make sure that the the surface is level and smooth. Sprinkle the top of the cake with a little demerara sugar.

4 Bake for about 1½ hours, until risen, golden brown and firm to the touch. Cool in the tin for a few minutes, then turn out on to a wire rack to cool completely. Serve in slices.

NUTRITION NOTES	
Per portion:	
Energy	278kcals/1175kJ
Protein	6.56g
Fat	8.08g
Saturated fat	2.16g
Carbohydrate	48.55g
Fibre	2.60g
Added sugar	16.95g
Sodium	0.16g

Cheese and Pineapple Wholewheat Scones

These cheese and pineapple scones are delicious eaten freshly baked, either warm or cold, as you prefer.

INGREDIENTS

Makes 14–16

225g/8oz/2 cups self-raising
   wholemeal flour, sifted
5ml/1 tsp baking powder, sifted
a pinch of salt
40g/1½oz/3 tbsp polyunsaturated
   margarine
5ml/1 tsp mustard powder
75g/3oz/¾ cup reduced-fat mature
   Cheddar cheese, finely grated
50g/2oz/¼ cup ready-to-eat dried
   pineapple, finely chopped
150ml/¼ pint/⅔ cup skimmed milk

1 Preheat the oven to 220°C/425°F/ Gas 7. Line a baking sheet with non-stick baking paper. Sift the flour, baking powder and salt into a bowl.

COOK'S TIP

For economy, grate the cheese finely so it will go further and you will use less.

2 Rub in the fat until the mixture resembles breadcrumbs.

3 Fold in the mustard powder, cheese and pineapple and stir. Add milk as needed to make a fairly soft dough.

4 Turn the dough on to a lightly floured surface and knead gently. Roll out to a thickness of 2cm/¾in.

5 Using a 5cm/2in fluted cutter, stamp out rounds and place them on the prepared baking sheet.

6 Brush the tops of the scones with a little milk and bake them for about 10 minutes, until they are well risen and golden brown. Transfer the scones to a wire rack to cool and serve either warm or cold.

NUTRITION NOTES

Per portion:

Energy	99kcals/418kJ
Protein	4.22g
Fat	3.62g
Saturated fat	1.05g
Carbohydrate	13.28g
Fibre	1.74g
Added sugar	1.33g
Sodium	0.06g

Date and Orange Slices

These tempting, wholesome slices are moist and chewy.

INGREDIENTS

Makes 16

350g/12oz/2 cups pitted dried dates,
   finely chopped
200ml/7fl oz/scant 1 cup freshly
   squeezed orange juice
finely grated rind of 1 orange
115g/4oz/1 cup plain
   wholemeal flour
175g/6oz/1¾ cups rolled oats
50g/2oz/½ cup fine oatmeal
pinch of salt
175g/6oz/¾ cup half-fat spread
75g/3oz/⅓ cup soft light brown sugar
10ml/2 tsp ground cinnamon

1 Preheat the oven to 190°C/375°F/
Gas 5. Put the dates in a saucepan
with the orange juice. Cover, bring to
the boil and simmer for 5 minutes,
stirring occasionally.

VARIATION

Ready-to-eat dried apricots or prunes used
in place of the dates in this recipe make
equally delicious slices.

2 Stir in the orange rind and set aside
to cool completely.

3 Lightly grease an 18 x 28cm/7 x
11in, non-stick cake tin. Put the
flour, oats, oatmeal and salt in a bowl
and mix together. Lightly rub in the
half-fat spread.

4 Stir in the sugar and cinnamon.
Place half the oat mixture into the
base of the prepared tin and, using the
back of a spoon, press it down firmly.

5 Spread the date mixture on top and
sprinkle the remaining oat mixture
evenly over the dates to cover them
completely. Press down lightly. Bake for
about 30 minutes, until golden brown.

6 Allow to cool slightly in the tin and
mark into 16 fingers, using a sharp
knife. When firm, remove the slices
from the tin and cool completely on a
wire rack. Finally, break the cooked
fruit and oatmeal cake into fingers.

NUTRITION NOTES

Per portion:

Energy	197kcals/829kJ
Protein	4.02g
Fat	5.76g
Saturated fat	1.48g
Carbohydrate	34.06g
Fibre	1.76g
Added sugar	5.25g
Sodium	0.08g

Lemon and Raisin Rock Cakes

These lightly spiced, fruity rock buns are easy to make, and delicious to eat.

INGREDIENTS

Makes 16
225g/8oz/2 cups self-raising
  wholemeal flour
a pinch of salt
115g/4oz/½ cup half-fat spread
115g/4oz/generous ½ cup golden
  granulated sugar
5ml/1 tsp ground mixed spice
finely grated rind of 1 lemon
115g/4oz/⅔ cup raisins
1 egg, beaten
skimmed milk, to mix
pared lemon rind, to decorate

1 Preheat the oven to 200°C/400°F/ Gas 6. Line two baking sheets with non-stick baking paper and leave aside. Put the flour and salt in a bowl and lightly rub in the half-fat spread until the mixture resembles breadcrumbs.

2 Add the sugar, spice, lemon rind and raisins to the flour mixutre and mix together.

3 Stir in the egg and enough milk to make a stiff, crumbly mixture.

4 Using two spoons, put rough heaps of the mixture on to the prepared baking sheets. Bake for 15–20 minutes, until lightly browned and firm to the touch. Transfer to a wire rack to cool. Serve decorated with lemon rind.

——— NUTRITION NOTES ———

Per portion:	
Energy	126kcals/531kJ
Protein	2.90g
Fat	3.64g
Saturated fat	0.96g
Carbohydrate	21.69g
Fibre	1.41g
Added sugar	7.55g
Sodium	0.06g

Prune and Nut Teabread

Prunes, hazelnuts and walnuts make a successful partnership in this satisfying teabread, which is also highly nutritious.

INGREDIENTS

Serves 12

350g/12oz/1½ cups ready-to-eat
   pitted dried prunes, chopped
175g/6oz/¾ cup soft light
   brown sugar
300ml/½ pint/1¼ cups cold
   brewed tea
1 egg, beaten
50g/2oz/½ cup hazelnuts, chopped
50g/2oz/½ cup walnuts, chopped
225g/8oz/2 cups self-raising
   wholemeal flour
50g/2oz/2½ cups bran

1 Put the prunes, sugar and tea in a bowl and mix together. Cover and leave to stand for about 4 hours, until most of the tea has been absorbed by the fruit.

--- NUTRITION NOTES ---

Per portion:

Energy	223kcals/944kJ
Protein	5.53g
Fat	6.77g
Saturated fat	0.67g
Carbohydrate	38.17g
Fibre	5.28g
Added sugar	14.77g
Sodium	0.02g

2 Preheat the oven to 180°C/350°F/ Gas 4. Lightly grease a 900g/2 lb loaf tin. Add the egg, nuts, flour and bran to the prune mixture and, using a spoon, mix thoroughly.

3 Turn the mixture into the prepared tin and level the surface.

4 Bake for about 1¼ hours and insert a skewer to check that the teabread is cooked throughout. Cool in the tin for a few minutes, then turn out on to a wire rack to cool completely. Serve the teabread cut into slices.

Cheese and Herb Wholewheat Soda Bread

Full of flavour, this delicious, savoury bread should be served freshly baked.

INGREDIENTS

Serves 8

350g/12oz/3 cups plain
  wholemeal flour
115g/4oz/1 cup fine oatmeal
10ml/2 tsp bicarbonate of soda
10ml/2 tsp cream of tartar
2.5ml/½ tsp salt
115g/4oz/1 cup reduced-fat mature
  Cheddar cheese, finely grated
45–60ml/3–4 tbsp chopped fresh
  mixed herbs
2.5ml/½ tsp mustard powder
300ml/½ pint/1¼ cups buttermilk
water, to mix
30ml/2 tbsp skimmed milk
15ml/1 tbsp medium oatmeal

1 Preheat the oven to 200°C/400°F/ Gas 6. Lightly grease a baking sheet. Put the flour, fine oatmeal, bicarbonate of soda, cream of tartar, salt, cheese, herbs and mustard powder into a bowl and mix together.

2 Stir in the buttermilk and enough water to make a soft dough.

3 Lightly knead on a floured surface. Shape into a 20cm/8in round.

4 Place the round of dough on the prepared baking sheet, brush the top with milk and sprinkle evenly with medium oatmeal.

5 Mark the top into eight even wedges. Bake for 30–40 minutes, until well risen, firm to the touch and golden brown.

6 Allow to cool on a wire rack. Break the soda bread into wedges to serve, and eat either warm or cold, as you prefer.

NUTRITION NOTES	
Per portion:	
Energy	251kcals/1063kJ
Protein	13.46g
Fat	4.84g
Saturated fat	1.87g
Carbohydrate	40.94g
Fibre	5.18g
Added sugar	0.00g
Sodium	0.25g

INDEX